THE DESIGN ACTIVIST'S HANDBOOK

THE DESIGN ACTIVIST'S HANDBOOK

How to Change the World
(Or at Least Your Part of It)
With Socially Conscious Design

NOAH SCALIN + MICHELLE TAUTE

HOW BOOKS
Cincinnati, Ohio
www.howdesign.com

For more excellent books and resources for designers, visit www.howdesign.com.

16 15 14 13 12   5 4 3 2 1

ISBN-13: 978-1-4403-0874-1

Distributed in Canada by Fraser Direct
100 Armstrong Avenue
Georgetown, Ontario, Canada L7G 5S4
Tel: (905) 877-4411

Distributed in the U.K. and Europe by F&W Media International, LTD
Brunel House, Forde Close, Newton Abbot, TQ12 4PU, UK
Tel: (+44) 1626 323200, Fax: (+44) 1626 323319
Email: enquiries@fwmedia.com

Distributed in Australia by Capricorn Link
P.O. Box 704, Windsor, NSW 2756 Australia
Tel: (02) 4577-3555

Designed by Noah Scalin
Layout by Noah Scalin, Kim Phillips, Gina Kang
Unless otherwise credited, images and illustrations copyright Noah Scalin.

Edited by Amy Owen
Art directed by Grace Ring
Production coordinated by Greg Nock

ACKNOWLEDGMENTS

A big thank-you to everyone who submitted work for the book, took the time to talk with us, and offered up advice, leads and/or encouragement.

DEDICATION

For all the students who have taken my Design Rebels course in the graphic design department at Virginia Commonwealth University. — *Noah Scalin*

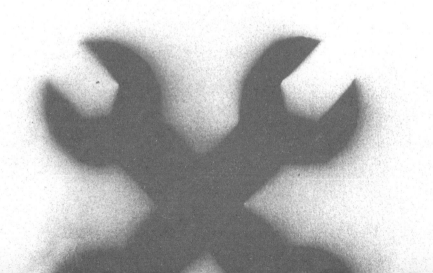

TABLE OF CONTENTS

FOREWORD

BY DAVID BERMAN

Students in the 2010
Design Rebels class at
Virginia Commonwealth
University created this
installation to show
the average waste
most people generate
annually and how much
of it could be reused
and/or recycled.

**Hey, fellow designers. You're about to spend some
quality time with Noah Scalin and Michelle Taute.**
If you haven't met Noah before, I'm pleased to be
the one who gets to introduce him to you, because
he and I are common souls.

Noah is dedicated to inspiring young designers to
make the world better. I first met him in 2004, at
a pub table in Richmond. I was in town to speak
to students at Virginia Commonwealth University,
where Noah teaches a class called Design Rebels,
and we've been talking about our shared passion for
design activism ever since.

I've been to over fifty countries and have met a lot of inspiring designers: designers eager to make a difference. But I've never seen anyone deliver a book like this one, where the authors actually lay out, step-by-step, how to turn your intent into action.

It's easy to dwell on the world's troubles, but we live in a truly remarkable time. As designers, we are the stewards of knowledge. And it has never been easier, never less expensive, never more immediate, to send messages over great distances to larger and larger populations.

In the past, most designers didn't have the wealth to publish their own material, so they were at the mercy of clients or employers to find projects that consisted of design products or messages that didn't just do good design, but did good. Today, the internet makes it possible for designers to "own a printing press." They can launch self-directed projects or businesses, with the internet as the means of distribution… or even the means of fabrication.

This book includes many examples of designers doing just that, and it gives every designer a glimpse into the strategies, techniques and passion it takes to turn ideas and daydreams into rewarding design activism.

The internet makes so much sharing possible. And yet as Nicholas Negroponte reminds us, for the majority of people alive today, the internet is still just a rumor. Only 30 percent of humanity has ever interacted with the internet. But over the next ten years that will change forever. Before this decade ends, most human beings *will* have had their first interaction with the internet.

So, will that first access to the internet be about sharing the best we have to share? Will it be about ideas like medicine, conflict resolution, wisdom, compassion standards, democracy, governance and free thought? Or will it be just one more way to convince ever-growing populations in the developing world that they "need" to consume stuff—way more stuff—in order to feel they belong in the global culture?

Will designers bring our best skills out to support goodness and truth? Or will we prop up the greed disorder of a minority by using our cleverness to help convince more and more people that they are not tall enough, thin enough, white enough, curly enough, cool enough?

Perhaps the internet provides us with our single most valuable opportunity in which to help build a better world. Indeed, we live in an age where everyone is a designer, and the future of civilization is our common design project. And this book ties the loftiest goals to practical next steps.

Friends, we have the opportunity to decide whether we will simply do good design or we will do good with design.

Noah and Michelle help us imagine what is possible if designers do not participate in the export of overconsumption and the unbridled fulfillment of greed. No one understands the powerful mechanism behind these manipulations better than design professionals, and we have the creativity and persuasiveness to make a positive change. We must act, be heard and sometimes simply say no by designing a better yes.

Are we too late? Not at all. The time is perfect. Two decades ago, if you said you were a graphic designer, people asked, "What's that?" Now they are asking: "What are designers really about? Are they tradespeople? Are they craftspeople? Are they artists? Professionals? Are they ethical? Responsible?" What are our answer going to be?

Design is a very young profession. We've barely begun. Over 95 percent of all designers who have ever lived are alive today. Together it is up to us to decide what role our profession will play. Is it going to be about selling sugar water, and smoke and mirrors to the vulnerable child within each one of us? Or is it going to be about helping repair the world?

Let's embrace a responsible and honored role in society. Once we do so, society will truly recognize the power of design and the special role that designers play in a brighter future. I know that if we fulfill the gifts of our professional skills by recognizing our power and the stewardship responsibility that accompanies that power, we can make a real difference. And since we can, we must.

And how to pursue such a lofty goal? We've all heard that every journey begins with one small step. You've taken that step by picking up this book. Now let Noah and Michelle provide you with all the steps that follow.

Intent into action. It's what they're about, and it's what we all need to be about.
So don't put down this book. Instead, let's get started.

David Berman, *Deputized Design Rebel*

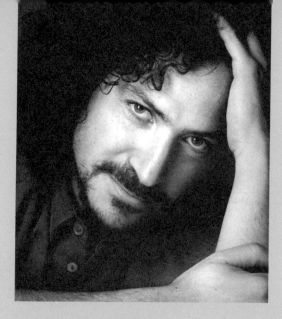

David Berman (www.davidberman.com) is a Canadian designer and thought leader. He is a board member of Icograda, the world body for graphic design; a fellow of the Society of Graphic Designers of Canada; and the ethics chair for graphic design in Canada. David has recently been named a special advisor to the United Nations on how to use accessible design thinking to fulfill the Millennium Development Goals. As an expert speaker, he has traveled to dozens of countries and is a national member of the International Federation for Professional Speakers who is also profiled with the National Speakers Association. If you want help establishing a Nobel Prize for design, please contact berman@davidberman.com. Read the first forty pages of his book **Do Good ~~Design~~** at davidberman.com/ dogoodgooglebook.

P.S. Are you still reading this foreword? You're supposed to have already gone ahead with the rest of the book. Get on it. Now. We need you to do this. Your grandchildren's children need you to do this. Your soul needs you to do this. Go, design rebels, go!

PREFACE

Noah Scalin: The Life of a Socially Conscious Designer

Do you want to be a hired gun who works for the highest bidder? Or to give a voice to people, causes and ideas that deserve to be heard? Noah created this image about freedom of expression for the international Poster for Tomorrow exhibition.

I attended my first protest rally in a stroller.

At least that's what my mom has told me. The first one I remember attending was a march for the Equal Rights Amendment when I was a little bit older. I wore a large "ERA YES" button while I roller-skated through the crowd. Suffice to say, I grew up believing that if you wanted social change you had to do something about it.

So it came as a bit of shock, years later when I grew up, to discover that I was expected to put these convictions away in the name of making a living (not my parents' expectations, mind you, but pretty much the rest of the world's). I guess I had always assumed that one's values and one's vocation would somehow align. But when I graduated college I was suddenly thrust into a world where people hung up their ethics on the way into the office—and that just wasn't acceptable to me.

Even though my father taught graphic design throughout my life, I did not consider it a career path for myself until I was already graduating college with a degree in theater design. Somewhere along the way I found that making posters for plays was far more interesting than actually creating the sets or costumes. But shortly after deciding to make a living from graphic design, I realized the job I loved contributed to some of the biggest issues that concerned me: creating mountains of waste, reinforcing negative stereotypes, polluting the air and water, and encouraging wasteful spending. Graphic design had a hand in the marketing and promotion of a destructive way of life that I had no interest in supporting.

So how could I make these seemingly divergent interests—doing good, making a living and doing something I loved—into a seamless whole? Since I was asking this question in the midnineties, there were not a lot of resources for discovering whether other people had similar concerns, and if so, what they were doing about it? So I decided to create an experiment. I would make the type of business that I thought needed to exist and see if it would actually work in practice.

At the first protest rally Noah remembers attending as a child, he wore a large ERA Yes button and roller-skated through the crowd.

In reality, there were many other people across the globe with similar concerns. All of us were working in our own bubbles, making it up as we went along, wondering if we were the only people who cared. In those early days I found inspiration in books like the seminal *Design for the Real World* by Victor Papanek, which is where I first encountered the term "socially conscious design." In his book, Papanek introduced industrial designers to a new way of thinking about their career, a field that he deemed one of the worst from a societal standpoint. What did he consider to be even worse?

"There are professions more harmful than industrial design, but only a very few of them. And possibly only one profession is phonier. Advertising design, in persuading people to buy things they don't need, with money they don't have, in order to impress others who don't care, is probably the phoniest field in existence today."

Talk about feeling guilty about my new career!

Then to my delighted surprise there was a sudden explosion of articles about socially conscious graphic design in the late 1990s. It seemed I wasn't alone after all, and I happily signed on to the newly rewritten First Things First Manifesto (see original page 30) and wrote a letter of encouragement to *Emigre* magazine after they dedicated an entire issue (*Emigre* 49 1999) to how designers could address social issues. Sadly this heyday was short-lived. When I proposed more articles about socially conscious design, one magazine told me, "We've already written about that," as if having ethics were only a fad to be replaced by the next hot topic the following season. And in a way they were right. The attention of the masses shifted to other things, but in its wake a lot like-minded folks discovered they were not alone and began to connect and share experiences and knowledge online.

Even so, when I finally made the jump from working full-time as an in-house graphic designer to running my own socially conscious firm, there were plenty of people who thought I was crazy. Again and again I was told, "That's nice, but how are you going to make a living?" Of course, that was generally preceded by, "You're starting a what?" It was early in 2001 when I made the leap and terms like "corporate social responsibility" and "triple bottom line" (see page 41) were still not commonly used. Of course the term "greenwashing" (see page 130) wasn't that well known yet either.

It was in this climate that I began my grand experiment. I named my socially conscious design firm Another Limited Rebellion, Incorporated, as a way of both thumbing my nose at the system that I was trying to transform and acknowledging my own hubris in attempting to do so. I created a short list of ethical principles that the business would follow (see page 38) and set out to prove the naysayers wrong.

Now here I am more than ten years later. And if the results of my experiment can be measured by the simple fact that my company still exists all this time later, it has been a success. I still have a roof over my head. And refusing to work on projects that compromise my beliefs has brought me more work, not less. Actually, I'd call all that a rousing success.

Best of all, I'm now far from being alone on this journey.

I set up my company not only as a means to make a living doing what I love while doing good, but as a model to show others it was possible for them to take the same path. In that vein, I have been teaching a course on socially conscious design at Virginia Commonwealth University called "Design Rebels: Socially Conscious Design in Theory & Practice" since 2003. In the class, my students are introduced to the ethical gray areas that designers have to confront when they begin to work in the "real" world. They are also introduced to the powerful tools of persuasion that are in their hands. Then my students are presented with the choice I hope you will consider as well: Will you act like an assassin? Someone highly trained to kill and willing to shoot whomever they are asked to point their gun at if the price is right. Or will you be like a megaphone? Raising the voices of those who need to be heard above the din.

This book is really an extension of my class: an introduction to the concept of making a choice to work from an ethical perspective and the practical aspect of making a living while doing so. Consider yourself a newly deputized Design Rebel and dive in.

– *Noah Scalin*

"THE FUTURE IS AN INFINITE SUCCESSION OF PRESENTS, AND TO LIVE NOW AS WE THINK HUMAN BEINGS SHOULD LIVE, IN DEFIANCE OF ALL THAT IS BAD AROUND US, IS ITSELF A MARVELOUS VICTORY."

–HOWARD ZINN

INTRODUCTION
MAKING A DIFFERENCE AND MAKING A LIVING

Everywhere you turn in the design world people are talking about "doing good."
There's a never-ending supply of blog posts, magazine articles, books and conference talks. Looking for inspirational eye candy? Images of gorgeous nonprofit projects are a mouse click or page turn away. Not sure why all of this is so important? It's easy to read up on why designers should apply their talents to world ills like poverty, global warming and overconsumption, but no one tells you, in practical terms, how to make socially conscious design part of your day-to-day work life.

Sure, one of those "rock star" designers might suggest you take on the occasional pro bono project or sign a pledge about your good intentions. But what if you feel like the only person at the office who cares about this stuff? Or a huge corporation that you don't feel 100 percent good about offers you a ton of cash for a freelance project?

These are tough situations for those who worry about paying the rent or making the mortgage and finding affordable health insurance. And that's a big part of why we decided to write this book. It's for every designer who's ever sat at a computer, thinking: Is this it? Isn't there more? We set out to help graphic designers figure out how to start making a difference and making a living—no matter where they live and work right now. It's time to translate all this talking and thinking into meaningful, widespread action.

WORK

MAKING A DIFFERENCE

SLEEP

Are you trying to spend your nights and weekends making up for what you do during the day? We think there's a better way to spend your 24/7.

MAKING A DIFFERENCE

SLEEP

Being a design activist means aligning your career with your values, so you're making a difference during that 40 to 60 hours a week you spend at work. Not trying to squeeze in what matters around the edges.

For starters, we believe socially conscious design is far too important to shove into those slivers of time left after work, sleep, family and a little fun. You shouldn't spend your weekends trying to make up for what you did at work all week. Doing good is too important to think of as work better left to those fictitious "other" designers. People more famous. More talented. More connected. Richer. Younger. Braver. (Insert your own mental roadblock here.) In truth, anyone can be a design activist. It just starts with a commitment to yourself and your values.

In the pages that follow, we'll take you through a process for defining your own professional ethics as a designer and using those guidelines to make the right choices for you. You'll also find stories and ideas from dozens of design activists that show you what a socially conscious design career actually looks like. Those folks told us not only what they do, but how they make it all work, from paying the bills during tough times to getting buy-in from traditional clients.

There isn't one set career path for socially conscious designers. We talked to people making a difference working in-house, primarily for nonprofits, at their own firms and freelance. Some of them even created their own product lines and founded nonprofit organizations on the side. Others combine two or more of these models to find the right balance for them between making a living and making a difference.

We've also included many tools and resources to help you affect positive change. There are tips on applying for grants, being an activist without getting fired and staying educated on pressing issues. At the end of every chapter, you'll find some questions and next steps to help you move forward on your own design activist path.

DEFINING A MOVEMENT

For all the discussion about "doing good," it's still a pretty vague concept with a lot of different names: green design, socially conscious design, socially responsible design, or as Milton Glaser prefers, *designism*. We believe a common language is crucial for transforming all this passion into a unified movement. Throughout the book we use the term "socially conscious design," because we believe it most accurately encompasses all the issues that might concern a design activist, from the environment and workers' rights to racism, sexism and more. We refer to people practicing socially conscious design in their daily lives as "design activists."

Now, for the bigger question: What exactly is socially conscious design? It's about being aware, or as the Buddhists might say, finding a right livelihood. It's simple stuff like being honest and not causing harm to other living things. But at the most basic, it's a commitment to making conscious choices and realizing how all the decisions you make as a designer affect other people and the planet. It's about being awake instead of sliding by with the way things have always been done.

Socially conscious designers stay present and in the moment. They look at every job, every client as an opportunity to make the world a little better. It means taking a look at where and how you work and whether those decisions support your personal ethics or work against them (more on that in chapter 1). Living in a smaller city might give you more freedom to say no to clients you don't feel good about. Downsizing your lifestyle might do the same. Even steering clients away from stock photography that reinforces gender stereotypes helps change society.

Finally, we want to acknowledge that change is slow. It isn't going to happen overnight, but it is possible. It's happening right now, because of all the activists out there in every profession putting forth sustained effort and optimism even when nothing seems to be going their way. You might not get the grant the first time you apply, and you might not convince even half your clients to go for greener materials. As John Emerson, a longtime designer, writer and activist put it to us, "Social change can take a long, long time, and it's easy to get discouraged. Just don't give up."

WE WANT YOU: WILL YOU JOIN THE RANKS OF DESIGN ACTIVISTS?

All you need to do is say yes. Then we'll help you start walking in the right direction. It doesn't have to be perfect. Little actions from a lot of people add up to big change. This isn't a contest about who's the greenest or the most radical. You can slowly turn a job that isn't quite right into something you want to do. Or you can work from the inside to educate one of those big corporate clients about better choices. The goal is for everyone to begin moving toward a better model and to celebrate the small victories along the way. The sooner you start, the sooner change happens.

$147,273

Median salary for charity executives.

$42,400

Median salary for graphic designers.*

JUST SAY NO TO PRO BONO

When you're working with a nonprofit, it's tempting to volunteer your time and expertise. After all, they're doing good stuff, right? And you want to help them make that positive change happen. But just consider: Nonprofits are not no-profits. In a 2010 study of just over three thousand U.S. charities (conducted by Charity Navigator), the median salary for executives was $147,273 in 2008. Some nonprofit CEOs make a half million a year or more. These same groups also shell out big bucks for rent, computers, staff, consultants and more. So why should design and strategy be free?

It shouldn't—at least not as a default setting. We won't achieve a viable, widespread socially conscious design movement if we're all giving it away for free. And that's why most of the design work in this book stems from paid client engagements. We're not saying there's never a place for pro bono; some groups truly are no-profit. But we encourage you to attach a clear value to your skills whenever possible. You might trade advertising with an indie radio station or offer an annual grant of your services (learn more about giving grants on page 74). Even charging a nominal fee to scrappy activists trying to bootstrap an effort helps them see you as a strategic partner (see more about sliding fees on page 56).

*Sources: Bureau of Labor Statistics and Charity Navigator

THE IMPACT OF ONE LITTLE BROCHURE

Think you don't have much impact as a designer? Think again. Every choice you make impacts an interconnected web of people and natural resources. Here's a look at what happens before your brochure hits a consumer's hands.

YOU (THE DESIGNER)

YOUR STOCK PHOTO

Does it reinforce harmful stereotypes?

Or embrace a broader, healthier view of society?

YOUR PRINTER

Is it someone who helps you make sustainable choices?

Are the workers treated fairly and paid well?

Does the company make socially conscious business choices?

YOUR PAPER

Was the forest sustainably managed?

Or clear cut and forgotten?

How far did it travel to reach you?

Does it contain some recycled materials?

Are they pre- or post-consumer waste?

YOUR INK

Do the ingredients make you worry?

Or did you choose something healthier for the environment?

THE MAILING LIST

Is it unwieldy and untargeted?

Or does it contain only the right people for the message?

THE PRODUCT OR SERVICE YOU'RE PROMOTING

Is it something you feel good about and might use?

Or does it give you that bad feeling in your stomach?

NEXT STEPS

Okay, so now what? For starters, give a little thought to where and how you work.

Do you dream about working for yourself? Or do you prefer to have an employer?

☐ I want to be my own boss   ☐ I prefer a traditional job

Is the city where you live (or your lifestyle) so expensive that it limits your career choices?

☐ Yes   ☐ No

If yes, what changes are you willing to make to give yourself more freedom?
I'm willing to:

☐ Move to a cheaper neighborhood or city

☐ Move to a less expensive house or apartment

☐ Cut monthly extras like cable

☐ Give up my car for a bike and/or public transit

☐ Consume less, experience more

☐ Rethink the idea that success = a bigger salary

Name three things that make you feel good about your job:

1.

2.

3.

And three that tug at your conscience:

1.

2.

3.

DESIGN

living. So, seen from a communications pers[...]
problems are really design problems. That's [...]

Take a look at the voting experience map bel[...]
ways you can put design to work for democra[...]

A COMMUNICATIONS MAP OF THE AMERICAN VOTER'S EXPERIENCE

EDUCATION	REGISTRATION	PREPARATION	NAVIGATION	VOTING
LEARNING ABOUT VOTING RIGHTS AND DEMOCRACY	SIGNING UP TO BECOME A REGISTERED VOTER	BECOMING INFORMED AND PREPARED TO VOTE	FINDING THE WAY TO THE VOTING BOOTH	INDICATING A CHOICE IN AN ELECTION

EDUCATION

WORD-OF-MOUTH

Families are a primary source of civics education, but this method of voter education is inadequate.

HIGH SCHOOL CIVICS CLASSES

We learn about voting rights in high school civics classes, which are disappearing from U.S. education.

CITIZENSHIP CLASSES

Laborious self-study books are replacing the traditional citizenship classes required for naturalization.

REGISTRATION

PAPER REGISTRATION FORMS

Complicated, badly printed voter registration forms are common in most states.

ONLINE REGISTRATION FORMS

Oregon Voter Registration

Download a Voter Registration Form now! English vers[...]

Many states are testing on-line registration systems. To minimize fraud, most states still print out a paper form.

MOTOR VOTER APPLICATIONS

Many states allow for voter registration on the driver's license application, but the check boxes can be hard to find.

VOTER ROLLS

Many voters are turned away from the polls because their registration is incomplete or inaccurate.

PREPARATION

SAVE-THE-DATE CARD

To maintain our records accurately, it is important THAT YOU R[...] CARD TO US if the person to whom it is addressed no longer [...]

Everything you need to know is often lost on the poorly-designed voting reminder postcard sent to every home.

VOTER REGISTRATION CARD

Each voter gets a registration card to tell them where to vote. Can they find it on election day? Maybe not!

PUBLIC SERVICE ANNOUNCEMENTS

VOTE

Non-profits produce get-out-the-vote campaigns during elections, but they need more money and design help.

PRE-ELECTION INFO PROGRAMS

Welcome to the 2001 Primary Election Voter Guide

Pre-election information packages come in the mail, but get lost or buried in piles of junk mail.

CAMPAIGN LITERATURE

Many voters rely on political campaign literature to prepare for elections. It is accessible, but is it objective?

SAMPLE BALLOTS

Sample ballots can help voters to rehearse and plan what they will do in the voting booth.

NAVIGATION

EXTERIOR STREET SIGNS

ELDERLY AND HANDICAPPED VOTERS RESERVED PARKING

VOTER PARKING ONLY

Clear and legible temporary directional signs are needed to help voters find their way to the precinct door.

PRECINCT SIGNAGE

VOTE HERE

Temporary signs turn public buildings into precincts. They are often too small and poorly-designed to be effective.

LINE AND BOOTH IDENTITY

42 ELECTION DISTRICT

How many voters waste time standing in the wrong line? Inadequate signage design and placement is often to blame.

PRECINCT WORKERS

Most voters depend on precinct staff to help them navigate the precinct.

CAMPAIGN WORKERS

Voters look for campaign workers as a signal that they are approaching the polls, but they are unreliable.

VOTING

HAND-COUNTED PAPER BALLOT

SONIA JOHNSON, Virginia and RICHARD J. WALTON, Rhode Island — Citizens' Party
LYNDON H. LaROUCHE, JR., Virginia and BILLY M. DAVIS, Mississippi — Independents

Paper ballots list all choices on a sheet of paper. They are easy for the voter to use, but hard to tabulate.

MACHINE-COUNTED PAPER BALLOT

DEMOCRATIC PARTY
WALTER F. MONDALE of MN. and GERALDINE A. FERRARO of N.Y.

This ballot is like a standardized test. It is designed for machine tabulation and not for voter ease-of-use.

MECHANICAL LEVER

These complicated machines make it easy to tabulate votes, but many voters find them difficult to use.

PUNCHCARD

82	120	158	196	234	272	310	348
83	121	159	197	235	273	311	349
84	122	160	198	236	274	312	350

The voter puts a ballot book over this punch card and pokes a selection. Sometimes it works, sometimes not.

DIRECT RECORD ELECTRONIC

New ATM-like voting machines are coming, but the interfaces need extra design attention to ensure ease-of-use.

VOTING INSTRUCTIONS

Pull the red voting handle from left [...]

palanca grande de color rojo desde la izquierada

Even the best voting technology won't work if the user instructions are confusing or hard to figure out.

DESIGN PROBLEM	DESIGN PROBLEM	DESIGN PROBLEM	DESIGN PROBLEM	DESIGN PROBLEM
DISAPPEARING CIVICS CLASSES	FORMS THAT ARE BARRIERS TO PARTICIPATION	TOO MUCH OR TOO LITTLE INFORMATION	GETTING TO THE BOOTH ON TIME	USER-UNFRIENDLY VOTING MACHINES

DESIGN TO THE RESCUE

HOW YOU CAN GET INVOLVED

ALL KINDS OF DESIGNERS

GRAPHIC DESIGNERS can help by designing voter [...]

THERE IS WORK TO BE DONE

1. BECOME A POLLWORKER in your own precinct

4. CALL YOUR CONGRESSPERSON ABOUT [...]

or not votin
sy
or emergency
terested
town
like candidates
eason

st source of voter expe-
en and why people vote

what is on the voter's
voting process.

SURVEYS

ou to get here

ou to vote?

he

rarely done but are
tter voting process.

EM
EMENTS
PUT

1. THE ACTIVIST'S TOOLBOX

As a design activist, you're an agent for social change.

You can wield your professional skills to work on issues you're passionate about, whether that means bike lanes or better public education in your city or starting a recycling program at the office. But on an average day, the whirlwind of deadlines, meetings, bills, family and everything else can make you feel less powerful than you are. It's easy to get stuck in the status quo and start thinking: How much influence does design really have anyway? This chapter takes a stab at answering that question and offers up three activist tools to help you put your passion to work.

Think design doesn't have much influence? Sylvia Harris, who headed up Citizen Research & Design, created this poster to illustrate all the places where design impacts the voting process. Client: University of Minnesota Design Institute.

TOOL 1
RECOGNIZING DESIGN'S POWER

"Designer" might not be the most natural job title for someone who wants a career focused on social change. But design does have enormous power to influence, persuade and inform. Think that's an exaggeration? Just step inside your mental time machine and go back to the Bush vs. Gore presidential election in 2000. All those confusing ballots and hanging chads in Florida should be coming back to you right about now. It's not a stretch to say that design— or in this case the lack thereof—may have changed that election's outcome. If there had been a clearer, more functional ballot, would Al Gore have become president? And perhaps adopted the Kyoto Protocol to limit greenhouse gas emissions? We'll never know, but it's a reminder of how much power stems from design, both good and bad.

On a daily basis, design, advertising and branding play a sizable role in defining our shared culture. They help determine what we buy, how often we buy it and our vision of "normal," from income to body type and gender roles. Many of us who work in the industry like to think we're somehow above all of these influences. But are we really immune to the ad spend? According to a study of 2010 U.S. advertising spending done by Kantar Media, Procter & Gamble spent $3.1 billion, General Motors $2.1 billion and AT&T $2.1 billion. Would companies shell out all that money for advertising if it didn't work?

Keep in mind that those figures are for a single calendar year and just

Design has the power to give people a voice and help them come together, turning a group of people into an organized protest. Lincoln Cushing created these images for a slide show promoting his book Agitate! Educate! Organize! American Labor Posters (Cornell University Press, 2009). Learn more at: www.docspopuli.org

a handful of companies. Add up the ad spend of the Fortune 500 alone, and it's hard not to believe all those dollars are changing the way we think and act. In a 2007 study published in the Archives of Pediatrics & Adolescent Medicine, preschoolers thought identical food offerings like fries, carrots and milk tasted better when offered in a McDonald's wrapper vs. plain packaging. (Though, somewhat surprisingly, hamburgers were a toss-up.) A 2003 study conducted at Harvard found that pharmaceutical companies increased drug sales by $4.20 for every $1 they spent on direct-to-consumer advertising. In some cases, people are not even recognizing ads for what they are. A 2011 study published in *The Journal of Advertising* found that children didn't know online games that contained advertising for food companies were ads at all—even when there were labels pointing out the promotion.

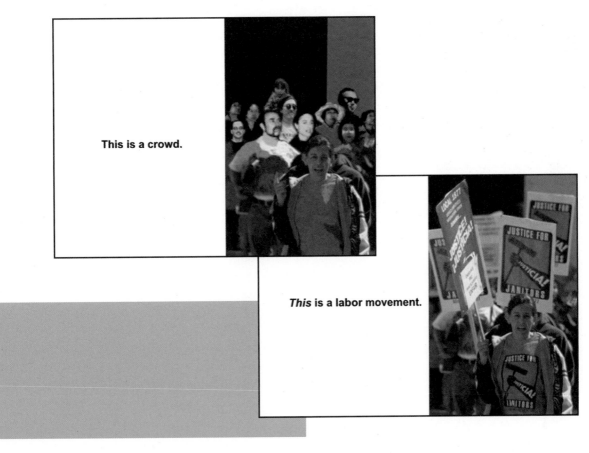

This is a crowd.

This is a labor movement.

FIRST THINGS FIRST

A MANIFESTO

Socially conscious design might feel like a relatively new topic, but designers have been thinking about how to craft careers that make a difference for decades. Writer and designer Ken Garland published "The First Things First" manifesto back in 1964 and twenty-one fellow creatives signed it. It calls into question the notion that advertising is the highest pursuit for designers and photographers. In 2000, an update on the classic manifesto appeared in a number of magazines as a whole new generation took up the call. But we think the original text (republished below with permission from Ken Garland) applies more than ever:

We, the undersigned, are graphic designers, photographers and students who have been brought up in a world in which the techniques and apparatus of advertising have persistently been presented to us as the most lucrative, effective and desirable means of using our talents. We have been bombarded with publications devoted to this belief, applauding the work of those who have flogged their skill and imagination to sell such things as:

cat food, stomach powders, detergent, hair restorer, striped toothpaste, aftershave lotion, beforeshave lotion, slimming diets, fattening diets, deodorants, fizzy water, cigarettes, roll-ons, pull-ons and slip-ons.

By far the greatest effort of those working in the advertising industry are wasted on these trivial purposes, which contribute little or nothing to our national prosperity.

In common with an increasing number of the general public, we have reached a saturation point at which the high-pitched scream of consumer selling is no more than sheer noise. We think that there are other things more worth using our skill and experience on. There are signs for streets and buildings, books and periodicals, catalogues, instructional manuals, industrial photography, educational aids, films, television features, scientific and industrial publications and all the other media through which we promote our trade, our education, our culture and our greater awareness of the world.

We do not advocate the abolition of high-pressure consumer advertising: this is not feasible. Nor do we want to take any of the fun out of life. But we are proposing a reversal of priorities in favor of the more useful and more lasting forms of communication. We hope that our society will tire of gimmick merchants, status salesmen and hidden persuaders, and that the prior call on our skills will be for worthwhile purposes. With this in mind we propose to share our experience and opinions, and to make them available to colleagues, students and others who may be interested.

Edward Wright	Bernard Higton	Ivan Dodd
Geoffrey White	Brian Grimbly	Harriet Crowder
William Slack	John Garner	Anthony Clift
Caroline Rawlence	Ken Garland	Gerry Cinamon
Ian McLaren	Anthony Froshaug	Robert Chapman
Sam Lambert	Robin Fior	Ray Carpenter
Ivor Kamlish	Germano Facetti	Ken Briggs
Gerald Jones		

DESIGN + ACTIVISM IN HISTORY

The current socially conscious design movement is not an anomaly. Graphic designers have been using their skills for social change for nearly as long as the field has existed. Here are a few art movements that included graphic design as part of an activist arsenal:

ARTS & CRAFTS MOVEMENT

A rejection of the burgeoning age of mass production and the mistreatment of workers. Supporters worked to elevate respect for craftspeople and the materials they used in service of beautiful, functional design.

LATE 1800S – EARLY 1900S

Fortunately, design's impact isn't limited to complicating elections and pushing consumer goods. It also has the power to give a voice to people and causes without access to multimillion-dollar advertising budgets and to offer people alternative visions of how the world might be. "I think real change comes from empowering people to express themselves, to come together, to kind of reconceive of themselves in different ways," says John Emerson, a longtime designer, writer and activist who lives in New York. "Design has a very important and powerful role."

REALITY CHECK

How many planets would we need if everyone on Earth lived the same lifestyle as you?

Find out here: www.MyFootprint.org

P.S. We hope you score better than we did.

> **Noah:** ●●●●◖ 4.4 planets
> **Michelle:** ●●●●●◖ 5.4 planets

DADAISM

Artists enraged by the horrors of World War I create an anti-art that questions the established society that allowed it to happen. Most of the art forms they pioneered, such as collage and ready-mades, are still in use today.

EARLY 1900S

RUSSIAN CONSTRUCTIVISM

A rare movement where artists were in support of the government rather than against it. Constructivists worked to create functional art for the average person in all aspects of life.

EARLY 1900S

TOOL 2
CLAIMING YOUR POWER

Designers don't have the power to click a few computer keys and change the industry overnight. But you can start affecting positive change today by making more intentional choices. "When people talk about socially conscious design or socially responsible design, I think the biggest component of that is mindfulness and conscientiousness and just being aware of what you're doing and why you're doing it," says Jess Sand, former owner of Roughstock Studios in San Francisco. "The desire to really look at your own actions, the implications of your actions and who it affects both on a direct immediate level and the community at large."

SITUATIONISM

A small movement that has had
a big impact in recent years.
Situationists encouraged a rejection
of the mass spectacle of consumer
culture by using street art, reworked
advertising and pranks to
help people experience
the world in new and
unexpected ways. Their
legacy includes punk,
Adbusters, The Yes Men
and Improv Everywhere.

LATE '50s to EARLY '70s

All those little decisions you make every day about messaging, images, format, paper,
printers (and more) influence a vast, interconnected web of people and natural resources.
Pull on one little string—say the paper you choose—and you'll see that it affects a lot more
than the obvious:

- Where was that paper made?
- How were the people in the factory treated and paid?
- Where did the energy come from to run that factory?
- Did the raw materials for the paper come from a sustainably managed forest? Or
  would they have otherwise been industrial waste?
- How far did the paper travel to get to the printer? How was it transported?
- Does the message you're printing on that paper help or hurt people and the planet?
- What happens when your project's useful life is over?

The troubling questions pile up quickly, and they extend far beyond the umbrella of green
design. To make a difference, you need to take this bigger picture of socially conscious
design into account as you make decisions. You'll need to answer questions like these for
every project (see our sample project checklist on page 42), and doing that effectively means
staying informed. You can't make better decisions if you don't keep up with the issues, and
finding straightforward, factual information is tougher than it sounds. Do you trust the
companies that make the paper, inks and computers to give you unbiased information about

FLUXUS MOVEMENT

The ultimate rejection of art as something that belongs to the elite. Their DIY (Do-It-Yourself) anti-art mind-set picked up where the Dadaists left off and encouraged a rejection of traditional societal views of the world and a merging of art and life into a single whole. While not overtly political, many of the artists were aligned with the antiwar movement of the time.

1960S to PRESENT

their products? And how they're made? Or do you seek out independent data to double-check key claims?

Staying up on broader social, political and science news requires a skeptical approach, too. There may be more choices than ever for getting news and information, but only a handful of companies own the many media outlets. And these powerful media owners influence which issues get covered and whether it's done with a softball approach or critical in-depth reporting. Just one ownership example to consider: News Corporation's holdings include Fox News Channel, *The Wall Street Journal*, HarperCollins, Dow Jones, *New York Post*, FoxSports.com, more than a dozen local Fox TV stations, FX, 20th Century Fox Fox Searchlight Pictures and countless other media producers in the United States and abroad.

To start working around the system, here are a couple of good tactics for expanding your media horizon and putting together a truer picture of any issue:

1. Compare foreign news coverage, such as the BBC or *The Guardian*, to U.S.stories for a broader viewpoint and a reminder at how the rest of world sees us.
2. Look for news outlets that send their own reporters into the field instead of printing what everyone gets off the wire services.
3. Read and browse your way through the resources compiled in A Design Activist's Education on page 39 to raise your activist IQ.

THE IMPACT OF ONE LITTLE BROCHURE

Your impact as a designer doesn't stop once a piece is printed. It impacts a range of people and environmental factors after it leaves your hand. Make a practice of considering each project's end life while you're designing.

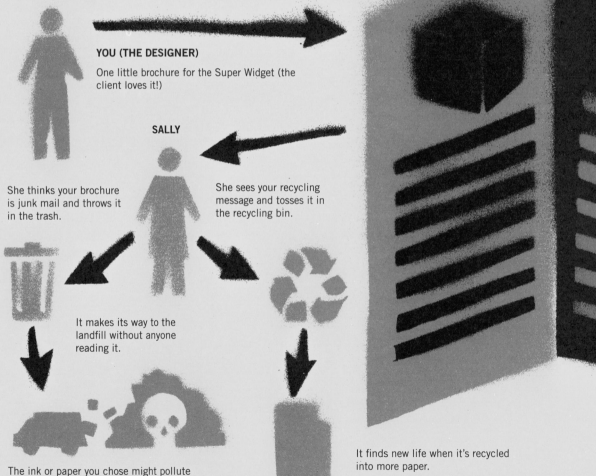

YOU (THE DESIGNER)

One little brochure for the Super Widget (the client loves it!)

SALLY

She thinks your brochure is junk mail and throws it in the trash.

She sees your recycling message and tosses it in the recycling bin.

It makes its way to the landfill without anyone reading it.

The ink or paper you chose might pollute the soil and groundwater.

It finds new life when it's recycled into more paper.

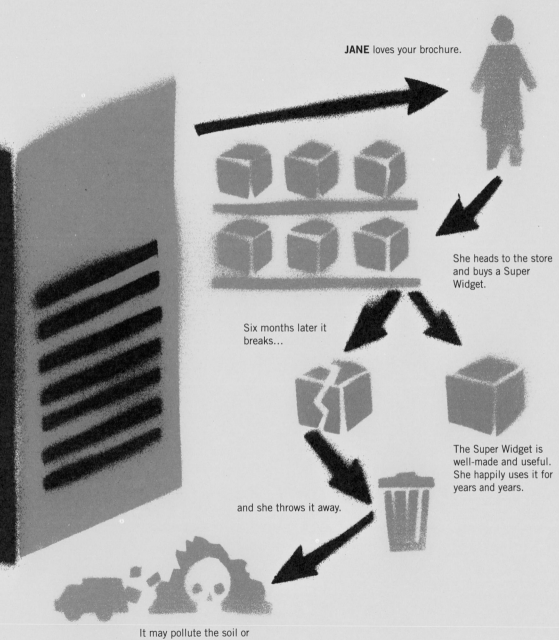

JANE loves your brochure.

She heads to the store and buys a Super Widget.

Six months later it breaks...

The Super Widget is well-made and useful. She happily uses it for years and years.

and she throws it away.

It may pollute the soil or groundwater.

TOOL 3
DEFINING PROFESSIONAL ETHICS

The word *ethics* tends to come off as academic and authoritarian, but ultimately professional ethics are just a formalized gut check. They're a personal statement about what you will and won't do at your job, and a framework for seeking out clients, projects or employers that are a good match for your beliefs. We encourage every design activist to think through and write down a set of personal ethics, so something is in place to guide you when you run into a sticky situation while racing against four different deadlines.

We're not going to tell you what your ethics should be. No one can define them for you, and they'll most likely evolve over time. But we've included examples of other designers' approaches here as inspiring thought starters. My coauthor, Noah Scalin, runs his company, Another Limited Rebellion, based on a multipoint philosophy that outlines key ethics:

- Provide high-quality design for clients whose work benefits the communities in which they are located.
- Work with clients who are not involved in the creation of cigarettes, alcohol or weapons.
- Work with companies that are not involved in a labor dispute nor are targets of a boycott for its labor or environmental practices.
- Attempt to make designs that create a minimum of waste and do as little harm to the environment as possible.

A DESIGN ACTIVIST'S EDUCATION

Noah's top ten resources for socially conscious designers (in no particular order):

Do Good ~~Design~~ by **David Berman**
This small volume covers the sins of branding and advertising in a personal, inspirational way. If you're hesitant to commit to design activism, this book offers plenty of reasons to change your mind.

A People's History of The United States by **Howard Zinn**
Want proof that small groups of committed citizens really can make a difference? Read this amazing history of America written from the perspective of working class men and women.

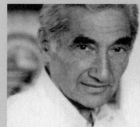

A PEOPLE'S HISTORY
OF THE
UNITED STATES

HOWARD ZINN

- Encourage clients to use environmentally sensitive printing processes and materials whenever applicable to a design.
- Create pro bono designs when possible for nonprofit organizations with extremely limited resources.
- Donate 10 percent of profits to nonprofit organizations.

The list is prominently displayed on the firm's website, which helps attract clients who share the same beliefs. These tenets also serve as a framework for the business. They're something to refer back to when figuring out whether or not to take on a particular client or how to execute a particular project. But it's important to keep in mind that professional ethics aren't foolproof. You may not be successful at sticking to them 100 percent of the time. And that's okay. The important thing is to make an effort. Doing something, even if it's small, is better than not trying at all.

No Logo by **Naomi Klein**
An eye-opening look at the effect of corporate interests on our culture. Rather than an activist rant, it's an incredibly well-researched critique of the rise of branded society. It's even more relevant today than when it came out in 2000.

The Christian Science Monitor
Despite the name, this paper is NOT about religion. Instead, it's one of the most well-respected sources of balanced original reporting in the world. **www.CSMonitor.com**

Mother Jones magazine
Hard-hitting, independently funded journalism featuring important social issues. Be prepared for articles that will raise your hackles about problems you've never even heard of before.
www.MotherJones.com

Social Design Notes
The grandfather of socially conscious design blogs. Spend a Friday afternoon sifting through the archives for hundreds of inspiring posts. **www.Backspace.com/notes**

Design Is the Problem
by **Nathan Shedroff**
A comprehensive overview of the systems available to help designers measure their work's sustainability. Plus, mini case studies on real-world products that are moving in the right direction.

The Age of Persuasion
In this entertaining Canadian radio show, an advertising industry insider takes a lovingly critical look at the history of commercial persuasion.
www.cbc.ca/ageofpersuasion

Osocio
An amazing and continually growing online collection of social marketing campaigns from across the globe. Get inspired, find out which design approaches work or just discover new issues to care about. **www.Osocio.org**

Re-nourish
A one-stop online resource that helps designers reduce their environmental impact: case studies, a calculator for reducing paper waste, independent info on environmentally responsible printing and paper choices, and more.
www.Re-Nourish.com

Find a more complete list in the Resources section on page 171.

Sticking to your ethics might mean turning down clients or projects other firms wouldn't think twice about. Designer Jess Sand, who ran a solo practice for six years in San Francisco, researches the details before taking projects on. She might decide not to design a direct-mail postcard if a bloated mailing list means most of them will go straight to the trash. And when she received a phone call from a potential client interested in having her design a "green" website, it took detailed questioning to discover the site's purpose was actually a pyramid scheme aimed at environmentalists. She politely declined to bid.

Sometimes standing up for your beliefs comes with real professional risk. Before starting JusticeDesign in San Francisco, Jason Justice banded together with co-workers at a print shop and refused to create an anti-union brochure. The united effort forced the company to turn away the project, and the designers kept their jobs despite a district manager's threats. "I think it's important to stand up for yourself," he says. "Just follow your own moral compass. That's what I do more than anything else. If it's wrong to me, then I need to say something about it."

TRIPLE BOTTOM LINE = PEOPLE + PROFIT + PLANET

It's not all about the money. Activists everywhere owe a debt to John Elkington, who coined the term "triple bottom line" in 1994. The phrase defines a loose framework for measuring the broader success of a business. Are the working conditions good for people? How about the products or services themselves? And how does the business affect the Earth? All three factors—people, profit and planet—count toward a triple bottom line. For design activists, it's a great concept to introduce to clients or consider as you measure the success of your own business.

A PERSONAL CHECKLIST FOR WORKING WITH A BRAND

by Daniel Green, Green Bay, WI

☐ First, the brand must do no harm. Personal responsibility by the user has to be factored in here to a reasonable degree.

☐ The brand must be honest. If branding is about creating a relationship with the customer, dishonesty will ultimately betray and ruin that relationship.

☐ The brand keeps its promises. A brand is often defined as a promise, so if the promise is broken, so is the brand.

☐ The brand must never exploit– people or places–either in its production, its promotion, or its use.

☐ The brand must take responsibility. Mistakes or blunders do happen. Does the brand own up?

☐ Final litmus test: How eager would I be to wear the brand on my clothes when among friends and family?

At Another Limited Rebellion, Noah Scalin takes on pro bono projects for what he considers no-profits instead of nonprofits. This poster was created for the nearly all-volunteer community radio station WRIR in Richmond, Virginia. Instead of money, the station gave him underwriting spots on the air, which added a perceived value to his design work.

WRIR CELEBRATES 5 YEARS!
A PARTY FOR THE REST OF US
HEHS ORKEST · AMAZING GHOST · THE HOTDAMNS · LONG ARMS
PHOTOSYNTHESIZERS · BLACK LIQUID · TURNSTYLE SOUNDSYSTEM
FRIDAY FEB 5TH · 7PM - MIDNIGHT · RENAISSANCE BALLROOM 107 W BROAD

97.3 WRIR

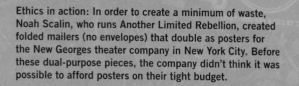

Ethics in action: In order to create a minimum of waste, Noah Scalin, who runs Another Limited Rebellion, created folded mailers (no envelopes) that double as posters for the New Georges theater company in New York City. Before these dual-purpose pieces, the company didn't think it was possible to afford posters on their tight budget.

Deciding who you won't work with doesn't have to be limiting. Instead of specializing in clients who are already focused on activism, Another Limited Rebellion often makes a difference by working with people who care about the issues but don't know how they might make a difference with their business. This dynamic often plays out with his theater company clients, who he works with to create marketing materials that have a limited environmental footprint.

THE ROAD TO HELL

BY MILTON GLASER

A few years ago I had the pleasure of illustrating Dante's *Purgatory* for an Italian publisher. I was impressed by the fact that the difference between those unfortunates in Hell and those in Purgatory was that the former had no idea how they had sinned. Those in Hell were there forever. Those in Purgatory knew what they had done and were waiting it out with at least the possibility of redemption, thus establishing the difference between despair and hope.

In regard to professional ethics, acknowledging what it is we do is a beginning. It is clear that in the profession of graphic design the question of misrepresenting the truth arises almost immediately. So much of what we do can be seen as a distortion of the truth. Put another way, "He who enters the bath sweats."

Finally, all questions of ethics become personal. To establish your own level of discomfort with bending the truth, read the following chart: 12 Steps on the Graphic Designer's Road to Hell. I personally have taken a number of them.

1 Designing a package to look bigger on the shelf.

2 Designing a package aimed at children for a cereal whose contents you know are low in nutritional value and high in sugar.

3 Designing a crest for a new vineyard to suggest that it has been in business for a long time.

4 Designing a jacket for a book whose sexual content you find personally repellent.

5 Designing a medal using steel from the World Trade Center to be sold as a profit-making souvenir of September 11.

6 Designing an advertising campaign for a company with a history of known discrimination in minority hiring.

7 Designing an ad for a slow, boring film to make it seem like a lighthearted comedy.

8 Designing a line of T-shirts for a manufacturer that employs child labor.

9 Designing a promotion for a diet product that you know doesn't work.

10 Designing an ad for a political candidate whose policies you believe would be harmful to the general public.

11 Designing a brochure for an SUV that flips over frequently in emergency conditions and is known to have killed 150 people.

12 Designing an ad for a product whose frequent use could result in the user's death.

DESIGN REBEL:

Mark Randall: Paying It Forward

LET'S START WITH THE CLIFFSNOTES VERSION: Worldstudio is a marketing and design firm that promotes social change at the grassroots level–both with clients and without them. In reality, it's hard to keep track of everything going on at this small studio. You might find the staff working on an identity for a Mexican restaurant or helping Warner Music Group figure out how to engage their employees in environmental issues.

There's also a full slate of self-directed projects, which Mark Randall, the firm's co-principal and creative director, describes as "showcasing possibilities." The efforts range from a scholarship program for minority and disadvantaged youth to Design Ignites Change, a nationwide program that encourages high school and college students to develop social change projects for their local communities. Many of these programs exist under the banner of Worldstudio Foundation, the design studio's nonprofit arm, and they're funded through a

> **"IF WE WANT DESIGN FOR SOCIAL CHANGE TO BE SOMETHING SUSTAINABLE, IT HAS TO GO BEYOND THE NOTION OF BEING PRO BONO. AND THAT'S SOMETHING WE REALLY FIRMLY BELIEVE."**

combination of grants, corporate partnerships and even some subsidizing by the firm's more traditional client work.

The five-person staff—three full-timers, two part-timers—budget their time into these social projects, but they often end up logging extra hours. When we talked with Randall, he was pouring much of his energy into a six-week program he put together for the School of Visual Arts in New York called Impact! Design for Social Change. It helps other designers figure out how to execute and fund their own social change projects and even puts students to work on real-world projects for local New York nonprofits.

What advice do you give designers who want to do good?
First, it has to start with a personal passion around a particular social issue or with a strong desire to want to contribute to positive social change. There are a couple of ways you can go about doing this. You can look for clients that might allow you to do this kind of work. And that's usually in the nonprofit realm. In many cases you will be hired to do a traditional design project like a brand identity or a brochure. Ideally you want to find a client that will allow you to push the envelope, to demonstrate how design can tackle social issues in innovative ways. Currently the mind-set isn't there for a nonprofit to hire a designer to do some kind of out-of-the-box design thinking project.

The other option is to create your own self-generated social change project. I find

For the *Create! Don't Hate* billboard campaign, high school students and their mentors design billboards that deal with issues of tolerance. A series of six billboards were showcased on the HD Spectracolor screen in Times Square, New York City. The project is an initiative of the Design Ignites Change program.

this to be the most exciting—and this is where your passion comes into play. If you have never done anything like this before the first thing I'd recommend is for you to look around your community and start local. You're not going to solve world hunger. Start small and be realistic. When approaching this type of work you have to be very entrepreneurial, this is something that designers are not as used to since design has traditionally been a service industry.

What else do socially conscious designers need to think about?

I think that the big missing link in the equation around doing self-generated social change work is funding. Designers are great at concept and at execution but the critical gap between those two is funding. There are many ways you can go about this, some of the ways in which we have done it is to leverage an existing client relationship, through corporate sponsorship and foundation grants, or through the sales of a product or service. There are a number of models that can be employed to support your effort. The other thing is to try and build into your funding plan compensation for the time that you put into your project. Don't just think of it

DESIGN TIMES SQUARE:
THE URBAN FOREST PROJECT

ROB ALEXANDER

TIMES SQUARE ALLIANCE

Worldstudio's Urban Forest Project engages local artists and designers to create artwork for light-pole banners using the metaphor of a tree. The banners here are from the inaugural Urban Forest Project in Times Square in 2006. (artist Rob Alexander). Other participating cities include: Denver, Baltimore, Albuquerque, Toledo, San Francisco and Washington.

Once the banners come down, they are up-cycled into a product and sold to raise money for local environmental initiatives. In this case, the product is a tote bag (right), designed by Jack Spade.

as a pro bono effort—especially if you want to make it a sustainable activity and you have limited means of support.

We find, too, that we have more success if we think of a project as a group effort, find partners and build a coalition. There is always strength in numbers. Also, once you have completed your project, measure its success and spread the word about what you have done. Create a case study which showcases your newfound capabilities in this area.

Do you think it's realistic for most designers to make their living doing socially conscious work?
There are many designers that work exclusively on projects for nonprofit organizations, which is a great place to start. But, as I mentioned, it often comes with limitations if you are interested in really expanding what designers can do in this area.

There will always be the need for all kinds of design. Somebody is going to design the BP oil company annual report, and I don't believe that there is anything wrong with that. I think what's really important is that if you are designing the BP annual report, you help shape the message, you don't allow them to greenwash or to misrepresent who they are. As the designer, try to work with your clients to get them to speak the truth. This is a way of being socially responsible, too.

Right now it is tough to create a design practice where you work exclusively on socially minded, self-generated projects. There are precedents in the product world. Take, for example, TOMS Shoes. It's a company that designs groovy shoes, and for every pair a consumer purchases, another pair is given to a child in need in a developing country. It's a fantastic for-profit social enterprise.

What Worldstudio accomplishment are you most proud of?
One of the things I'm most proud of is that we've been playing around with this model of design as a tool for social change for eighteen years. We were engaged in the idea long before it became popular; early on, we were referred to as those "do-gooders" over at Worldstudio. I'm also really proud of our scholarship program. We've given away nearly $800,000 to more than five hundred college students over the past fifteen years. And we're a tiny design studio. I think it goes to show that you don't have to be a big corporation or have a huge staff to make a difference.

www.worldstudioinc.com

NEXT STEPS

Set aside a few hours to consider and begin to define your own professional ethics (actually list them on paper). Start by reading—or perhaps rereading—Milton Glaser's "Road to Hell" (pages 46-47). Then take a look at the questions below:

Have you taken any of the steps on Milton Glaser's "Road to Hell?" Which ones?

Did they make you feel uneasy at the time?

How about now?

Are there things on the list you'd never consider doing? Which ones?

Reread the Brand Checklist on page 42. Do any of those sentiments ring true to you? If so, can you adapt them to your own ethical guidelines?

What will you do if you're asked to work on a project that doesn't match your ethics? When will you compromise? And when will you draw a hard line?

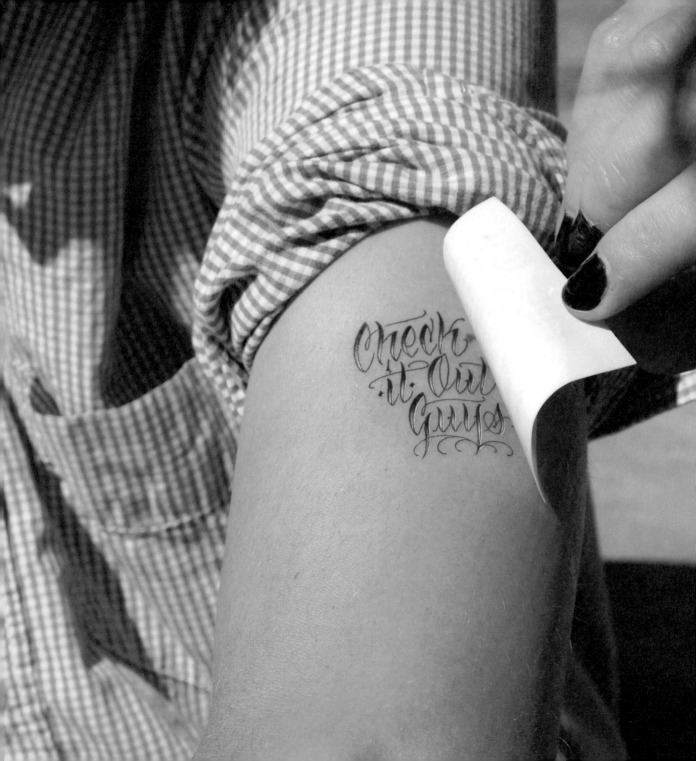

2. GOING IT ALONE

Two campaigns for Planned Parenthood Toronto, created by The Public, raised awareness that women who have sex with women and trans men need to have pap tests. The pieces used real people from these communities as models.

Of all the design activist career paths covered in this book, working for yourself might seem like the most obvious one. After all, you get to call all the shots: who you work for, the kind of work you do and how it all happens. But that's the challenge, too. Everything lands on your shoulders. For inspiration and advice, we sought out design rebels who are making it work, from one-person shops to firms with twenty-plus employees and offices on both coasts. This chapter addresses three key issues for activists running their own businesses: who your clients are, how you make ends meet and what goes into running an ethical business.

WHO YOU WORK FOR

Finding clients can be hard for any design firm, but it's especially tricky for a socially conscious one. Will you work exclusively with nonprofits? For businesses with do-good missions? Or with traditional companies that may need the most change? There's no one-size-fits-all answer, and it may take some experimenting to find the right mix.

When Lauren Bacon and Emira Mears started their web studio, Raised Eyebrow, in 2000, the partners focused on working with nonprofits. But during those early days, they actually did a lot of work for a real estate developer who was building condos in Vancouver. "A lot of our hard-core activist friends didn't really approve," Bacon says. "But I wouldn't trade that experience for the world, even if some of our friends thought we were selling out." The gig not only paid the bills, but it met the shop's criteria for working with clients outside their niche:

1. Are they awesome people to work with?
2. Is the working relationship respectful and engaging?
3. Will we be able to do really inspiring work that helps pay the bills?

THE SLIDING PAY SCALE

One tactic to help make ends meet: A sliding pay scale based on the size and type of client. A multinational for-profit corporation might pay your highest rate; a midsize nonprofit, a lower fee; and a group struggling to land their first grant, the least.

data(dot)gc.ca
a citizen-led beta for government data

Home   About   Data   FAQ   Feedback   How to Get Involved   Liberate a Data Set

Share This

Who's Sharing?

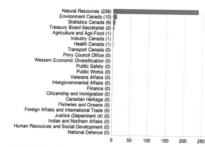

Natural Resources (238)
Environment Canada (10)
Statistics Canada (3)
Treasury Board Secretariat (3)
Agriculture and Agri-Food (1)
Industry Canada (1)
Health Canada (1)
Transport Canada (0)
Privy Council Office (0)
Western Economic Diversification (0)
Public Safety (0)
Public Works (0)
Veterans Affairs (0)
Intergovernmental Affairs (0)
Finance (0)
Citizenship and Immigration (0)
Canadian Heritage (0)
Fisheries and Oceans (0)
Foreign Affairs and International Trade (0)
Justice (Department of) (0)
Indian and Northern Affairs (0)
Human Resources and Social Development (0)
National Defence (0)

0 50 100 150 200 250 300

About this Site

Unlike the United States (data.gov) and Britain (data.gov.uk), Canada has no open data strategy. This must change. Canadians paid for the information gathered about our country, ourselves and our government. Free access to it could help stimulate our economy and enhance our democracy. In pursuit of this goal, this website is a citizen-led effort to promote open data and help share data that has already been liberated. Read more...

About the Graph

To encourage our government to share more structured data, this graph shows which ministries share and which do not. It is a powerful metric of how transparent a given ministry is.

Search datasets: ☐ Open license ☐ Downloadable   Go

Browse by:

Web design studio Raised Eyebrow focuses on online communications for nonprofits, such as the websites for the Canadian Association for Community Living and datadotgc.ca. "I think the social consciousness of what we do lies almost entirely in the work our clients do—not necessarily in our work per se," says partner Lauren Bacon. "We are supporting our clients' world-changing work."

PIVOT LEGAL LLP
a different kind of lawyer
a different kind of law firm

Home   About Us   Our Lawyers   Our Legal Services   Legal Resources

I went to law school to help ... and I am now at a firm th... doing just that.

Nina Purewal
LAWYER, PIVOT LEGAL LLP
PERSONAL INJURY CIVIL LITIGATION

OUR LAWYERS »
OUR LEGAL SERVIC
OUR PUBLIC SERVI

FREE LEGAL RESOURCES

LATEST ADDITION
...nadian International Adoption ...thorities
...sted by Anonymous on 23 Jul 2009

...w all resources »

...eed free legal advice?

PIVOT LLP EVENTS

No events have been added yet.

Sign In · Register Now

Home   About Us   CACL in Action   News & Stories   Publications & Resources   How You Can Help   CACL Foundation

50 years
Canadian Association for Community Living

Diversity includes.

10 STEPS TO INCLUSIVE COMMUNITIES

Equality Rights
Close Institutions
Child Rights
Family Supports
Inclusive Education
Disability Supports
Safe and Inclusive Communities
Eradicate Poverty
Employment Equality
Global Inclusion

OUR NEWSLETTERS

info@ news from CACL
keeping you informed
education watch
an update on inclusive education.
poverty watch
monitoring progress toward the eradication of poverty
coming together...
to create change
institution watch
monitoring progress towards deinstitutionalization

STAY UP TO DATE

✪ SUBSCRIBE TO OUR E-NEWSLETTERS
✪ CACL NEWS FEED (RSS)
✪ OTHER RSS OPTIONS

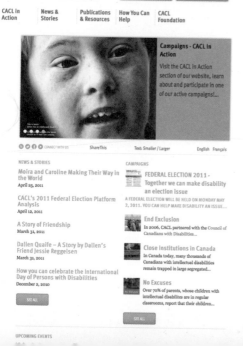

○○○○ CONNECT WITH US   ShareThis   Text: Smaller / Larger   English Français

NEWS & STORIES

Moira and Caroline Making Their Way in the World
April 25, 2011

CACL's 2011 Federal Election Platform Analysis
April 12, 2011

A Story of Friendship
March 31, 2011

Dallen Quaife – A Story by Dallen's Friend Jessie Reggelsen
March 31, 2011

How you can celebrate the International Day of Persons with Disabilities
December 2, 2010

SEE ALL

UPCOMING EVENTS

Campaigns - CACL in Action

Visit the CACL in Action section of our website, learn about and participate in one of our active campaigns!...

CAMPAIGNS

FEDERAL ELECTION 2011 - Together we can make disability an election issue
A FEDERAL ELECTION WILL BE HELD ON MONDAY MAY 2, 2011. YOU CAN HELP MAKE DISABILITY AN ISSUE...

End Exclusion
In 2006, CACL partnered with the Council of Canadians with Disabilities...

Close institutions in Canada
In Canada today, many thousands of Canadians with intellectual disabilities remain trapped in large segregated...

No Excuses
Over 70% of parents, whose children with intellectual disabilites are in regular classrooms, report that their children...

SEE ALL

HOME   OUR WORK   NEWS & MULTIMEDIA   PUBLICATIONS   EVENTS

British Columbia
Centre for Excellence
in HIV/AIDS
Together, we can stop HIV & AIDS

THERAPEUTIC GUIDELINES »
Up-to-date HIV treatment info

DRUG TOXICITIES »
Reactions and side-effects

REPORT A DRUG REACTION »
Patients and healthcare providers

Welcome to our new site!

Welcome to the British Columbia Centre for Excellence in H... have worked with staff and community partners to build this ... our work in treatment, research, and education with our regi...

In the coming months we look forward to rolling out new con... understanding HIV/AIDS in BC. If you would like to keep up ... by typing in your email address to the left of this screen...

Bacon says that client experience taught the pair a lot about running a business, valuing their skills and juggling multiple deadlines and priorities. "It also helped us get over our 'profit bad, nonprofit good' dichotomy attitude," she says. "We had a bit of a double standard as young, twenty-something entrepreneurs, where we had made an uncomfortable peace with running our own business, but 'big business' still seemed impersonal, vaguely threatening and sort of tainted." After this relationship, they realized that large companies are made up of individuals and that a lot of those people are trying to make the world a better place. And that it's important to apply your values and ethics to every situation, whether the client is for-profit or nonprofit.

For the National Crittenton Foundation, LeAnn Locher created this piece with a reusable jacket to inform expectant and parenting young single mothers in the foster care system about their rights. "You can design things that are beautiful and functional, and they'll be used and held on to," she says. "I don't want my work just thrown away and recycled."

Working with nonprofits means tackling sensitive issues. The campaign for the New York nonprofit Funders addresses racial equality in the LGBTQ community. "Just the term 'racism' we can't use because it automatically puts people on the defensive," says LeAnn Locher, president of LeAnn Locher & Associates. "All of the materials for the racial equality campaign were based upon question, answer and conversation."

In Portland, Oregon, LeAnn Locher, president of LeAnn Locher & Associates, runs a thriving business doing design and strategy work for nonprofits, public agencies and socially and/or environmentally responsible businesses. How does she make it all work? "I do what I say I'm going to do when I say I'm going to do it for the amount of money I say I'm going to do it for," she says. "Really, I think a lot of nonprofits have been burned by agencies or from people that fly by the seat of the pants, and I treat them really, really well." She's also intimately familiar with how nonprofits work and what challenges they face, because prior to going solo, she spent more than a decade at a PR firm specializing in this sector.

Many other socially conscious designers put together a living through a combination of clients: nonprofit groups, mission-based businesses and traditional corporations. In New York, freelance designer, programmer and writer John Emerson does a lot of work related to human rights advocacy and social justice, but he also occasionally works with traditional corporate clients. "I think it's case by case," he says. "You know, even when I worked with Human Rights Watch for three years as a staff member, there were positions they held that I didn't necessarily agree with. But I thought the work that they did was important."

MAKING ENDS MEET

For most people who dream of opening their own businesses, the biggest barrier can be summed up in one word: fear. "It was terrifying," says Sheila Sampath, about cofounding The Public, an activist design studio in Toronto. "There is money in corporate work. But it just wasn't sustainable for me anymore to work full-time and then come home and work full-time again to appease my conscience." Sampath gave up working as a freelance art director for ad firms, and her then partner, Una Lee, left a full-time corporate design job, so they could start a business together.

Both say their strong partnership helped them overcome those start-up fears, as did the knowledge that they'd be using their design talents for good instead of for profit. In fact, they believe the firm's strong focus on activist design has helped them attract the right clients and build a strong business niche. Another secret? Since they were both activists before designers, they're enmeshed in many of the communities their clients serve. This commitment helps them land work, understand clients and deliver effective solutions. "I think we both sort of independently realized that graphic design is a really powerful tool for social change," Sampath says. "And that we were probably much better as designers than we were as organizers."

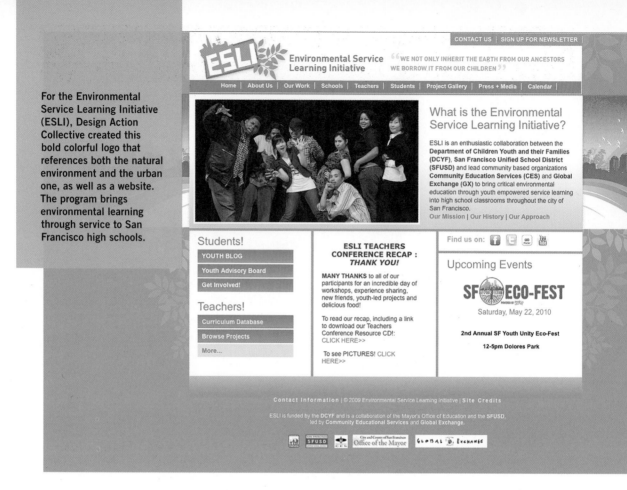

For the Environmental Service Learning Initiative (ESLI), Design Action Collective created this bold colorful logo that references both the natural environment and the urban one, as well as a website. The program brings environmental learning through service to San Francisco high schools.

We could fill this whole book with stories about designers successfully running socially conscious design businesses. It is possible. At Design Action Collective in Oakland, California, nine staff members (both designers and programmers) make a living primarily working with social change organizations, as well as some mission-based businesses. "We pay ourselves less than somebody who works for any commercial design firm as the principal," says designer Innosanto Nagara. "But we make a livable wage in the realm of what most of our clients make, people who work for nonprofits in the Bay Area." They also have full benefits and paid vacation.

BETTER BUSINESS MODELS

Certified

B Corporation™

bcorporation.net

B CORPORATIONS: In this modified corporate structure, the B stands for benefit and companies who bear the letter must live up to high standards for social and environmental conduct. There's also an effort under way to give B corporations legal standing in states across the country. A few certified B Corporations are: New Leaf Paper, Method, Dansko and Seventh Generation.

COOPERATIVES OR WORKER-RUN COLLECTIVES: This model democratizes the workplace by turning workers into owners of the business, and it's how Design Action Collective, an activist design firm in Oakland, California, operates. "You wear the hat of the board of directors as well as wearing the hat of worker here," says graphic designer Innosanto Nagara. "By having nine people who are all problem-solving together, who have an equal interest in the project succeeding, we do better."

STOP GAP
SWEATSHOPS

pro fleece vest
$29.50

Made by Cambodian
women earning $40/month.
The workers say they need
$60/month to meet their
basic needs.

original sweatshirt
$24.50

Made with indentured
labor here in the US,
on the island of Saipan.

carpenter cords
$29.50

The Chinese women who
work 12 hours a day making
these pants face being fired
or beaten if they complain.

ASK GAP TO PAY WORKERS A LIVING WAGE
AND TREAT THEM WITH DIGNITY

to learn more:
1-800-497-1994
www.globalexchange.org

64

But being an entrepreneur isn't always easy, and success can mean being open to change. Jess Sand founded her one-woman shop, Roughstock Studios, in 2004 but over the years, she found herself less interested in administrating the business and began to feel stifled by the solo nature of her practice. After much soul-searching, she took a seasonal in-house position at a local San Francisco nonprofit while continuing to freelance on the side. "My goal is to maintain control of the work that I do and to make my decisions conscientiously," she says. "If I can do that and still pay the rent, I have succeeded." Ultimately, Sand was offered a permanent communications position with another nonprofit, which she accepted. Having identified for so long as Roughstock Studios, she found moving in-house to be a difficult decision, but it meant she could continue to work with the issues that are important to her from within a larger team. In some ways, Sand feels she is able to have an even greater impact in this capacity.

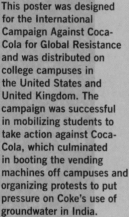

Coca-Cola

Destroying Lives, Livelihoods & Communities

· Depriving Communities of Drinking Water All Across India

· Poisoning the Groundwater and the Soil Around Bottling Plants in India

· Distributing Toxic Waste to Farmers in India as "Fertilizer"

· Selling Contaminated Drinks in India, with Pesticide Levels 30 Times Higher than US and EU standards

· Complicity in the Murder, Torture and Intimidation of Union Organizers in Colombia

Unthinkable! Undrinkable!

Join Us to Hold Coca-Cola Accountable for Human Rights, Labor and Environmental Crimes

www.IndiaResource.org

Design by Design Action Collective

This poster was designed for the International Campaign Against Coca-Cola for Global Resistance and was distributed on college campuses in the United States and United Kingdom. The campaign was successful in mobilizing students to take action against Coca-Cola, which culminated in booting the vending machines off campuses and organizing protests to put pressure on Coke's use of groundwater in India.

This cover for Left Turn magazine, created by Design Action Collective, was also sold as a poster to raise money. It celebrates the resilience of people in Detroit and Dakar, and promoted issues related to Africa and the African diaspora at the U.S. Social Forum.

FROM DETROIT TO DAKAR

YOUR BUSINESS'S ETHICS

When people talk about socially conscious design, the emphasis inevitably turns to clients. Are they good environmental stewards? How do they run their business? And treat employees? But it's important to turn these same ethical questions back on yourself. At the web design shop Raised Eyebrow, for example, they make a point to provide competitive salaries and benefits, all while sticking to a no-overtime rule for all staff. But these values can make it tough to compete with agencies that recruit unpaid interns and expect senior staff to log sixty hours a week. To stick with their core values, Raised Eyebrow must focus on efficiency and charge relatively high fees to combat their narrower profit margin.

Two campaigns for Planned Parenthood Toronto, created by The Public, raised awareness that women who have sex with women and trans men need to have pap tests. The pieces used real people from these communities as models.

It's also crucial to figure out when and how you'll draw boundaries with clients and potential clients. One of the first projects the women behind The Public competed for was the design of a teen magazine called Sex, etc. During the proposal process, they were asked to submit cover concepts without compensation, but instead, they included a long, thoughtful letter with their submission on why pro bono work is problematic. "For me, there was some hesitation about making that decision even though it was the right thing to do," Sampath says. "It could jeopardize the chance of getting this amazing job. But it would be the basis for this studio that didn't quite exist yet."

The Public created the branding for the 2009 convention for the Ontario office of the Canadian Union of Public Employees (CUPE). To portray the diversity of the membership, they used phrases and arrows that referenced the conference attendees themselves: "You are the solution. We are the solution. I am the solution."

INVEST IN PEOPLE

WE ARE THE SOLUTION

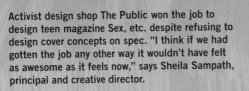

Activist design shop The Public won the job to design teen magazine Sex, etc. despite refusing to design cover concepts on spec. "I think if we had gotten the job any other way it wouldn't have felt as awesome as it feels now," says Sheila Sampath, principal and creative director.

The organization behind the magazine, called *Answer*, responded positively and agreed to pay The Public to submit covers. Ultimately, Sampath and Lee landed the job, and they believe this early decision to refuse pro bono work helped them start the relationship on the right foot. It's one of mutual respect and the exchange helped the client see The Public as not only designers, but activists and thinkers. In general, the firm strives for horizontal relationships with mutual respect and doesn't shy away from questioning clients as much as clients question them.

Some ethical questions to consider for your business: How green is your office? Do you want to work toward a more sustainable model? What do you want the work environment to be like? What do you want relationships with vendors and clients to be like? How do you feel about unions? Will you offer flexible schedules and the option to work from home? How many hours will your staff work each week? What about benefits?

A PRO BONO ALTERNATIVE:
AWARDING GRANTS

There are plenty of worthwhile groups out there that truly don't have the money for design services. And many of them are run by passionate people who believe in the same socially conscious things you do. So what's the most effective way to deal with pro bono requests and share your talent? One solution is to award a grant of your design services.

It's an approach used by a number of design firms, including Rogue Element in Chicago. In 2008, this small shop began the process of awarding yearlong grants that are worth roughly $50,000 in work. They've partnered with RACHNA (Research, Advocacy and Communication in Himalayan Areas), as well as an organization that's trying to start the equivalent of the Sierra Club in India and an organic dog biscuit company called Barkwheats. "A grant helped us legitimize what we were trying to accomplish for people," says Allison Manley, a partner at Rogue Element. "It really elevated us, and I highly recommend other design firms steal our idea."

Here are a few lessons learned from the firm's grant-giving efforts:

- Create a formal application process. Because it takes effort to apply for a grant, you'll attract groups who are serious, organized and more likely to make good use of your work.

- Choose a focus. Rogue Element wanted to work on environmental issues, so they opened their grant to people who work in that area. What issue do you want to be involved with?

- Funnel all pro bono requests to the grant. You'll save time by sending people to an online grant application. And focusing your efforts on one group allows you to help them build a strong brand instead of doing piecemeal work for a number of different organizations.

- Consider a board. Rogue Element leaves the selection of the grant winner to a board that includes professionals from the design, business and sustainability realms. This adds a level of accountability to the process and cuts down on ill will from rejected applicants.

RACHNA

Rogue Element created this logo for RACHNA (Research, Advocacy and Communication in Himalayan Areas) as part of a yearlong grant they awarded to the nonprofit.

DESIGN REBEL:

Jonah Sachs: Activism Goes Viral

IN 1999, JONAH SACHS COFOUNDED FREE RANGE STUDIOS OUT OF HIS APARTMENT WITH LOUIS FOX, HIS FRIEND SINCE AGE SEVEN. The pair shared a computer, and Louis slept and ate on Jonah's couch. But besides a desire to create truthful ads for good causes, the pair didn't have many worries beyond coming up with the $400 monthly rent. Today Free Range employs twenty-eight people, with offices in Berkeley, California, and Washington DC, and they're most well-known for provocative online videos like The Meatrix and The Story of Stuff series.

With genius storytelling and just the right amount of humor, these viral pieces explain the environmental and social problems behind factory farming, bottled water, cosmetics and more. The tone is compelling and empowering rather than depressing. The design firm's client list reads like a who's who of the nonprofit world: Amnesty International, Human Rights Campaign, The Nature Conservancy, Planned Parenthood and many more. But

> **"THE POWER OF DESIGN IS TO FUNDAMENTALLY CHANGE THE WAY PEOPLE SEE THE WORLD."**

they also work with traditional companies on select projects, including a series of videos for Autodesk, a software company that encourages engineers and designers to choose less-toxic materials.

What do you think about all the talk and attention right now being paid to "good design"?
To a lot of people do-good means community service stuff, or you know, a green version, 25 percent less plastic in our bottles. People are so removed from their idealism that they don't actually think speaking truth through design is a viable direction.

Mostly, I think it's still within that very dominant paradigm of "big corporations rule the world." This is where the money and the ability to do things are. That's where people are seeing do-good design. Really, the power of design is to fundamentally change the way people see the world. It can be disruptive. Story of Stuff is disruptive, and that's where my interest is.

I think it's great that designers are touching their idealism. But I think it needs to and can go a lot further. I feel like there's a lot of conflict among change making, design and putting the greenwashing sheen on things.

The online flick The Meatrix combines pop culture and humor with tough facts about factory farming. The film has racked up more than twenty million views and been translated into twenty languages. It also helped Free Range build a reputation as an online storyteller. www.meatrix.com

But I also think there are a lot more young people who are used to the fact that they can create and produce their own media. They don't need anyone to help them do it. They're coming out of these schools and are more willing to hold out for the projects that they want to do. I think that movement is awesome. This young generation is not necessarily so slavishly hoping to walk up the corporate ladder, and that might lead to some more radical stuff.

Do you think every designer can make a living as a socially conscious designer?
I think as long as there are products that we don't need in a society of overconsumption, there are always going to be designers who are part of that. Not everyone can be a socially conscious designer, but we can bring a positive spin to anything that we do.

We all see 3,500 ads a day. Now those ads are not going to necessarily be for good

Shareable is an online magazine that promotes sharing as a way to consume less while still enjoying life. www.shareable.net

products and things that we need. But the stories that we see are these advertisements. If they're constantly speaking to our lower selves and pushing our fear and greed and vanity and all those things, we're going to be a fearful, vain, greedy society.

Even with the same mix of products and the same horrible overconsumptive society, those ads could at least appeal to our higher natures and treat us like the potential-filled human beings that we are. If designers can step in and push towards a media landscape that's more respectful of individual human beings, I think that can make a positive change.

How often do you have ethical dilemmas at work?

The people who we wouldn't want to work with for the most part stay away from us. When they do call, they're pitching us instead of asking us to pitch them. Someone might call and say, "We know we're a giant mega food company, but here are the good things that we're doing." We'll ask ourselves 1) Do we support the activities of this company in general? And 2) Is it a social campaign in line with the kind of stuff that the company actually does? Or are they just trying to put a sheen on their actual activities?

We did a project for Clif Bar because we felt like the company was imbued with values about organic food. So we felt good about doing that. But we've turned down quite a few in the food world. We turned down a project with Dole to work on their organic side, and we've turned down a project with the Indian multinational corporation Tata, because they are building energy-efficient cars, but they're also building coal-fired power plants.

How tough is it to keep things going now that you have so many folks on staff?

We pride ourselves on giving good service and helping people who are trying to help the world in less revolutionary ways, too. So we're doing a major branding project for the National Hospice and Palliative Care Association. They're helping people die with dignity and that seems really important. It also takes a lot of our resources, and I wouldn't use it at all as a negative example.

The No Impact Project empowers people to change their lifestyles and significantly lower their impact on the environment. http://noimpactproject.org

But if we say, "What is our model for change? How do we see the world ultimately transforming in this urgent way?" We don't always have the luxury to only seek those clients out. So we have a lot of do-good clients that are not necessarily revolutionary. That compromise is, I think, valuable for the community of nonprofits and change makers out there. The ability to be completely reflective and totally be a for-profit ad buster is really hard. I don't think we've been able to fully stay on it. We subsidize our few superradical projects a year with a lot of do-good projects.

But we haven't had those really hard times a lot of companies have experienced. I think the only way to explain the fact that we've kept loyalty and kept work flowing is because we haven't tried to be something we're not. The more things get a little scary, the more I insist that we stay on focus, because that's the only way to explain the fact that we haven't had problems like that.

www.freerange.com

The Story of Stuff Project, an ongoing series of short online videos, takes on overconsumption and other social issues and simplifies complex topics in a way that doesn't dumb them down or take away the seriousness of the message. www.storyofstuff.org

THE STORY OF STUFF

WITH ANNIE LEONARD

NEXT STEPS

Starting a business—or refocusing the one you already have—is a big step.
Here are some things to help get you started:

Do you want to start alone or have a partner? Is your eventual goal to have
employees, or do you prefer to stay small?

Who will your clients be, and how will you find them?

What's a realistic time frame for going out on your own?

SOME TO-DOS:

- **SAVE MONEY.** It's going to take some time before your company becomes profitable—and you'll need to work out cash flow issues. Try to save a six-to-twelve-month safety net.

- **FREELANCE ON THE SIDE.** If your job allows, start building up your business chops and client lists by taking projects on the side. Working part-time and freelancing part-time is another good option.

- **WORK UP A ROUGH BUSINESS PLAN.** Head to the library or Amazon and check out some books on starting businesses and writing a plan. Then dig in.

- **COMMIT TO ONE THING A DAY.** It's intimidating to start a business and that fear can lead to procrastination. Carve out twenty or thirty minutes a day to work on your dream.

- **ASK FOR ADVICE.** Find some small business owners and freelancers you admire—even if they're not designers—and offer to buy them lunch in exchange for some advice.

- **PRICE INDIVIDUAL HEALTH INSURANCE** and look into options for setting up your own retirement savings account.

3. CLIENT WHAT CLIENT?

Designer Sheri L. Koetting gave up drinking bottled water, and in 2009, her firm created an environmental art installation called Watershed, which shows the negative impact of excessive plastic bottles. The display included 1,500 plastic water bottles, or one second of U.S. consumption.

Sometimes it can seem like your clients are standing in the way of what you really want to be doing. They're not buying into your most innovative ideas or aren't interested in the issues you're most passionate about. So what if you stopped thinking you needed a client to make your best ideas happen? There are ways to find funding for your projects or make them a reality on a shoestring budget. And these efforts almost always lead to something unexpected. This chapter covers founding a nonprofit, launching a product and pursuing self-directed design projects. Designers in the trenches describe the benefits and challenges of pursuing each approach.

FOUNDING A NONPROFIT

A lot of graphic designers dream about having nonprofit clients. But what if you founded your own nonprofit organization? One that addresses the issues nearest and dearest to your heart? In Portland, Oregon, Michael Etter works as an art director at Ziba design by day, doing design work for big corporate clients, and spends another ten to twenty hours a week running his nonprofit, re:active, Inc. The group works with teens that might otherwise be swept up by drugs or gangs to create a magazine roughly once a year, and sometimes other creative projects, too. "I am not trying to make magazine makers or designers necessarily," he says. "I am trying to get people interested in their own lives and what they want."

The nonprofit re:active works with teens to create themed magazines that give them an avenue for self-expression. For issue number 5, Portland teens wrote and illustrated re:define, Fear with help from mentors. Designed by Joshua Berger of Plazm.

re:active.mu

re:active issue no. 5

re:active
issue no. 5

re:define

DARKNE

milk

COMMUTE

DAIRKNE

AFRICA

COMMITMENT

Cute

9915-6
0015-0

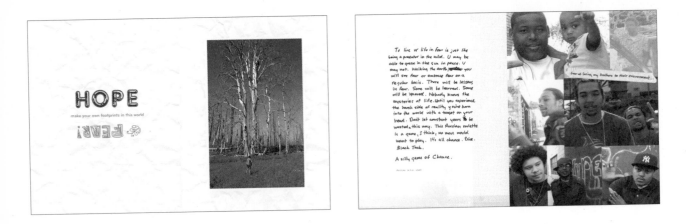

HOPE

make your own footprints in this world

¡FEAR!

To live ur life in fear is just like
being a predator in the wild. U may be
able to graze in the sun in peace. U
may not. Walking the earth, you
will see fear or embrace fear on a
regular basis. There will be lessons
in fear. Some will be learned. Some
will be ignored. Nobody knows the
mysteries of life. Until you experience
the harsh side of reality you're born
into the world with a target on your
head. Don't let constant years be
wasted this way. This Russian roulette
is a game, I think, no man would
want to play. It's all chance. Dice.
Black Jack.

A silly game of Chance.

Four at Soria, my brothers to their environment...

I feel like another person
because this is also my home
here,
there are no sidewalks
there are no buildings
the air is thinner and the breeze is longer and more cool
there are no buses no cars at all
no one showing off their twenty-inch chunks of useless shiny metal
there are no fingers being twisted into signs for honoring ignorance
and paying homage to disrespect
instead there are songs of hope and encouragement
there are no corners for pointless loitering or over-priced stores
here,
there is no need for money
the wind kisses the river
the sky is the river's twin
it's like the medicine for mama nature's sickness
I feel like another person
I left my sword and my shield at my other home
it's great to escape
where I can roam like my cellphone does here,
when I'm here
I'm home

Bo

These days Etter works with a four-person board (made up of himself and three others) and the benefit of full nonprofit status. But when he started the project in 2003, he was a design student in Los Angeles with few resources. After volunteering with incarcerated youths on a poetry project, he won his first grant (a Sappi Ideas That Matter grant) and produced a graphic book of the youths' poetry. He won some big awards with it and was encouraged to continue this kind of work. He decided to do something design and nonprofit related so he launched a magazine with a group of teens. The project has followed him through several moves, and he has kept it going with a hodgepodge of self-funding, grants and donations. Along the way, he has sought advice from people with similar projects, such as 826 Valencia, a writing program for kids in Los Angeles, and Worldstudio.

Spreads from re:define, Fear magazine show how creative and honest teens can be when given an outlet and a little encouragement. Photography by Paris Hart. Video stills and collage by Eloe Gill-Williams.

The folks at 826 Valencia let Etter take a look at their grant applications, volunteer hand-book and first contract for being fiscally sponsored. The latter is a good intermediary step if you don't have nonprofit status. Under fiscal sponsorship, a nonprofit organization agrees to take care of taxes and administration in exchange for a small percentage of your project's income. Help and advice came from other places, too. Worldstudio taught Etter about combining for-profit and nonprofit projects, and made corporate introductions that may eventually lead to funding. Even the owner of Ziba has offered Etter support, pointing him toward a lawyer who handled re:active's nonprofit status filing for free, as well as letting him have meetings during the week and use of the printer and other resources.

This billboard was created by mentor Kate Bingaman-Burt, famous for her daily purchase drawings, and student artist Patrick Prom.

Eventually, Etter hopes to pay himself for his time and have dedicated office space for the nonprofit. He also realizes his passion and energy can't support his vision alone, so he's working on surrounding himself with the right people—everyone from a CPA to curriculum developers. But he knows firsthand that you don't need all of that to get started. Instead of holding out for the perfect space or conditions, he urges designers to just go for it. "There are ways to start something on a grassroots level around you right now," he says. "There are people who would be interested in helping you even in small ways." He recommends you start by researching people and groups that are already doing what you dream of doing, so you can find mentors and avoid duplicating efforts.

LAUNCHING A PRODUCT

Here's another way to be a design activist: When you see a better way to do something, act on it. Allison Manley and Rob Coleman didn't think much about baby books until their young son began to chew on them in the summer of 2009. Then the designers, who co-own Rogue Element in Chicago, became concerned about everything from laminates, foils and glues to overseas printing. The pair didn't know exactly what materials were in their son's books, but their guts told them it wasn't all good stuff to stick in your mouth. "We were having a discussion about how terrible it was that there weren't any green children's books and Rob actually turned to me and said, 'Look, we're designers, why don't we just design some?'" Manley says.

And that's pretty much how the pair founded a second business called Squishy Press that creates nontoxic books for kids. They called up a photographer and started collaborating on the first two titles, *Opposites* and *Silly Faces*. As designers, they found that the conceptualization, shooting and layout were the easy parts. Then it was on to find the greenest materials possible: The couple was determined to make the books completely nontoxic, with little or no petroleum-based chemicals involved. "What we found interesting is that our vendors were just as interested as we were in coming up with a green product and communicating with one another about how to get there" Coleman says. "All of us were kind of making this up from scratch."

OPPOSITES

FIVE WAYS TO ROCK A GRANT APPLICATION

Every grant has different requirements and no doubt many applicants meet them, but we were curious about what sways the decision makers between one application and another. Armin Vit, of Principal UnderConsideration LLC, and one of the judges for the 2010 Sappi Ideas That Matter grants provided some tips and insight from the other side of the grant table:

1 Let your excitement shine through. Don't check your enthusiasm at the door. "Be passionate about what you are proposing," Vit says. "We could tell when someone had their heart behind it, and it pays off."

2 Be specific about how you'll spend the money. Show the judges you've done your homework when it comes to how much money you really need. Saying printing costs will be about $10,000 isn't as impressive as a printer quote with the exact price tag.

3 Tell a compelling story. Take a look at your application materials as a whole. Do they tell a good story about why your project is important and what impact it will have? Are they visually appealing? "It's very difficult to get people to imagine an end result and many applicants just couldn't get us there," Vit says. He says grant writing is an art form and practice makes perfect.

4 Choose your cause carefully. Judges are human and certain causes simply pull their heartstrings more than others. Take a look at all your project ideas and choose the one you believe will have the most impact when you apply for funding. "It's hard to NOT give money to an organization fighting poverty or women abuse," Vit says. "It's very easy to let your emotions and social priorities dictate who you select."

5 Cut out the fluff. There's limited grant funding to go around, so judges want to make sure every dollar counts. Go through your application and make sure you're asking for the essentials. Things like stationery, for instance, might not seem as important as the actual project you want to produce and deliver to an audience.

Total Heavy Metals Content (May 2010, First Printing of *Silly Faces* and *Opposites*)

	Antimony	Arsenic	Barium	Cadmium	Chromium	Mercury	Lead	Selenium
ASTM F963 Standard	60 ppm	25 ppm	1,000 ppm	75 ppm	60 ppm	60 ppm	90 ppm	500 ppm
Squishy Press Test Results	< 4.35 ppm	< 8.7 ppm	3.55 ppm	< 0.43 ppm	< 0.43 ppm	< 2.17 ppm	< 2.17 ppm	< 6.52 ppm

< = Less than   PPM = parts per million, and is equal to miligrams per kilogram (mg/kg)

To ensure their books are as environmentally and baby friendly as possible, the folks at Squishy Press paid to have a third-party laboratory test them for chemical content. They also freely share material choices on their website. The testing cost only a few hundred dollars, but the couple invested about $35,000 in the entire project—not including their time.

The printer, Lake County Press, put the couple directly in touch with TOYO Ink Group, and a lab tech there recommended an even greener ink than the printer had suggested. All the books were printed with a soy-based, low-VOC ink formulated without petroleum solvents. Mohawk Fine Papers ended up donating paper for the first run, because the company wanted to promote its Loop paper, which is made using 100 percent postconsumer waste and a chlorine-free process. Unlike other children's books that merely claim to be nontoxic, Squishy Press wanted to back up their claims, so they shared material choices on their website (www.squishypress.com) and paid to have the books independently tested for chemicals.

Why embrace so much transparency? "Part of it is that we want people to start doing this the same way we do it," Coleman says. "We want other book manufactures to start producing greener children's and babies books because our child is encountering these books, our friends' children, our relatives' children. We just think this is the right way to do things." The raw data about what's in the books also serves as a way to educate consumers about safety issues. So far, the hardest part of the whole project has been diving into the process of distributing a retail product. Manley and Coleman have had to learn about everything from bar codes and inventory to wholesale pricing.

PURSUING SELF-DIRECTED DESIGN PROJECTS

With your design skills and a computer, you determine how many projects you want to send out to the world. And many of them require more sweat equity than money. After founding Mark & Phil (it stands for marketing and philanthropy) in 2010, Sabrina and Daniel Schutzsmith didn't like how fast people were forgetting the ongoing Gulf oil spill. So the pair collaborated with Phil Buccellato and Jesse Ash of Greener Media (a video production studio out of Brooklyn) to create an online project called Instant Oil Spill. It lets anyone virtually spill oil over any website (without actually harming those sites). The project raised awareness, accumulating a million clicks, but it also showed off the firm's ability to execute effective design and strategy work around serious causes.

With video production help from Greener Media, Mark & Phil created the Instant Oil Spill project (www.instantoilspill.com), which lets you flood any site with oil to raise awareness about the 2010 Gulf oil spill. The self-directed project also raised awareness about the firm. When the cofounders show the project to new clients, usually someone in the room has already seen it.

Oxfam UK took notice of Instant Oil Spill and approached the firm to help them raise awareness about the lack of flood-related international aid to Pakistan. Mark & Phil and Greener Media created a flood version of the Instant Oil Spill project called Floodit.org (no longer live) and flooded the Oxfam UK site for a few days. The campaign prompted the British parliament to pledge more money to Pakistan and request that Oxfam UK take the flood site down. While the site didn't generate as much traffic as Instant Oil Spill, it reached the right eyeballs and led to the desired outcome.

At MSLK in Long Island City, New York, the cofounders started creating environmental art installations, which show things like the U.S. consumption of plastic water bottles every second (1,500) and worse yet, plastic bags (2,663), as a way to make a personal statement. "I think in the end we just needed to be in control of our destiny," says Marc S. Levitt, cofounder and creative director. "To make the kind of changes and impact we wanted, we just couldn't wait for our clients." As it turns out, these art projects have become a great conversation starter with the firm's clients in the beauty and fashion industry. And they've helped people with sustainability-related projects find their way to the firm. "It's led to more notoriety and exposure than anything else we've done," says Sheri L. Koetting, co-founder and strategist.

You don't have to wait for clients. MSLK in Long Island City, New York, started creating large-scale art installations to raise awareness about environmental problems on its own. This one focuses on those pesky plastic water bottles.

EACH SECOND 1500 PLASTIC WATER BOTTLES ARE CONSUMED IN THE US

Self-directed projects are also a great choice for engaging with your local community. The "I Dream of a Richmond ... " poster project actually came to designer and teacher Bizhan Khodabandeh in a dream. He used posters as a way to give regular people in Richmond, Virginia, free speech and empowerment. Photographers approached regular folks, asked them to complete the statement, give their name and age and pose for a quick photo. The resulting posters, roughly seventy in all, showed up all over town and in a local gallery show. "Some people don't start projects because they're afraid it might not work," Khodabandeh says. "I think it's really important to understand that you're going to make mistakes and that's okay." His project, for instance, originally asked for submissions, but he received almost none and decided to start working with photographers.

"I DREAM OF A RICHMOND that has more vegetarians and has less trash."

Kieryn, age 11

Bizhan Khodabandeh started the "I Dream of Richmond ... " poster project to give local people a true voice without the filter of the media. Photographers: Nick Kessler, PJ Sykes, Amanda Robinson and Karen Newton.

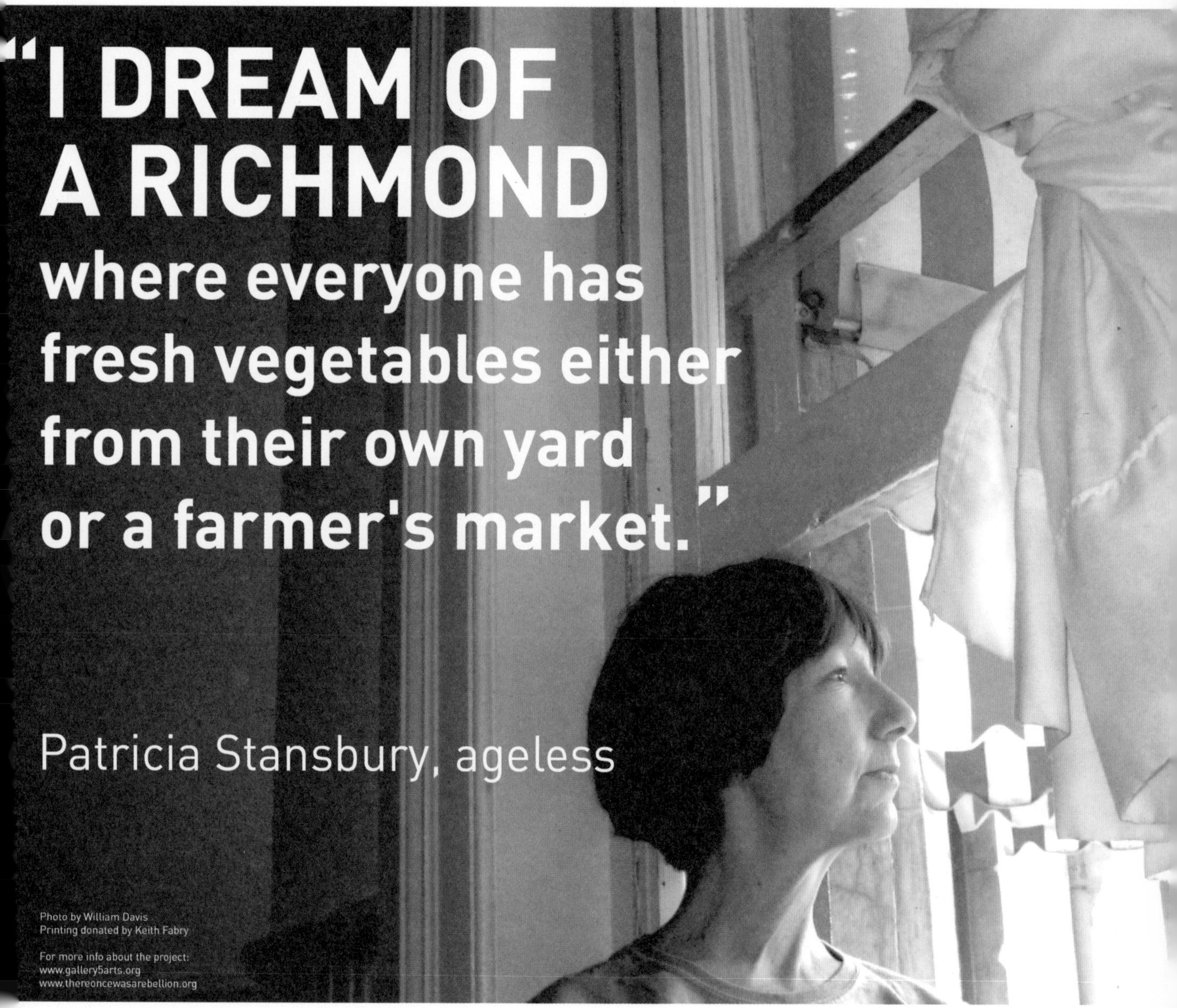

"I DREAM OF
A RICHMOND
where everyone has
fresh vegetables either
from their own yard
or a farmer's market."

Patricia Stansbury, ageless

Photo by William Davis
Printing donated by Keith Fabry

For more info about the project:
www.gallery5arts.org
www.thereoncewasarebellion.org

Benjamin Gaydos and Karen Stein from goodgood and photographer Matthew Shanley created the "We Will Imagine" project in the Fort Point district of Boston. They wove fluorescent tape through fencing to spell out "Who will imagine the future of all this? We will imagine." The project was meant to spark a dialogue and remind people of their own power and creativity.

So what's the secret to making a local project work? "Dialogue, dialogue, dialogue is most important," says Karen Stein, cofounder of goodgood, a design studio in Boston. "Don't feel like you're going to come up with a concept and develop it in your own little box because that will lead to an unsuccessful result." She and fellow cofounder, Benjamin Gaydos, have worked on a variety of self-initiated community projects, and they always make a point to get out and meet people—whether it's at the coffee shop or a local community group meeting. Try chatting with a diverse group of people—instead of just designers—and look at your efforts as long term. It takes a while to create a true partnership and dialogue within a community and things may not always move at your desired pace.

KEEPING A SELF-DIRECTED PROJECT ON TRACK

If you're like most creatives, your own projects all too easily get crushed on the bottom of the work pile. So how do you make your own ideas actually happen? The folks behind Squishy Press—Allison Manley and Rob Coleman—offer these tips:

- Treat it like a client project. This means following all the same steps and processes you would with any paying project from a client or your boss.

- Create milestones and stick to them. You need a set schedule and a to-do list to keep yourself on track. And approach tasks in the same order you would for a client job.

- Hold weekly or monthly meetings. Even if you are the only one who attends. These should be update meetings where you can check on milestones and reconfigure what isn't working.

- Introduce external deadline pressure. It's easier to stick with a deadline if someone else is expecting something from you. Squishy Press signed up to exhibit at a trade show, and it served as a deadline for finishing everything from the website to T-shirts.

DESIGN REBEL:

James Victore: Telling It Like It Is

IF YOU HAVE THE CHANCE TO TALK WITH JAMES VICTORE, DO SO. He doesn't disappoint. He's as energetic and honest as his work, and when you look deeper, you find a humbleness lurking beneath the big ideas and occasional cuss word. The artist and designer spends his time teaching at the School of Visual Arts in New York City, doing client work and creating a steady stream of self-directed projects.

All of Victore's work bears his unmistakable visual fingerprint, one that's earned him countless fans in the design community. Victore will tell you he's not an activist, but we think his bold and controversial work begs to differ. Enough about what we think. Nothing we could say about Victore is as interesting as what he says about himself and the design world.

> **"I KNOW THAT PEOPLE LIKE MY WORK, AND I AM TRYING TO FIGURE OUT HOW TO BASICALLY GET IT STRAIGHT TO THEM WITHOUT THE MIDDLEMAN."**

I heard you say in an interview that graphic design is a big club with spikes and that you wanted to wield it in the purest form. Can you talk about what you meant by that?

I look around at what I call commercial graphic design and it all just kind of looks alike. I can't really tell one artist from another or one company from another. You can't tell one fashion designer from another. It just seems like there's a lot of work that is being done because it has to be done. It's being done because we have to sell shit.

When I work for my heart, when I do something that I believe in, I am amazed at the reception that it gets. I am amazed at the amount of people who respond. But if we don't work like that, it's basically just pandering. I have zero interest whatsoever in designing a beer label to look like a fucking beer label or making a box of cookies look like it's supposed to be a box of cookies.

I don't know, I just think the brightest minds of our generation these days are being used to make buttons that people can push so they can buy shit. Or they're making basically candy.

I think graphic design is an amazing tool. I think it can be used to save the world, but nobody knows how and nobody is interested. We're all kind of distracted, and we're all good Americans, so we have two and three jobs. I mean, if I could pay my bills by being a teacher, that would be awesome, but it's impossible these days.

love, Victore

Advertisers think you're stupid.

love, Victore

Advertisers

"I like mantras that you mediate with and I believe in the power of slogans," Victore says. He came up with the phrase, "Advertisers think you're stupid," then ordered the stickers out of a catalog, calling in the color and size.

I think people look at you as someone who gets paid to do the work you want to do. How is that possible?

I think most creative people feel like that's not even an option. It's not impossible. It's just a line that I wanted to tow since the beginning, and I have been very lucky in finding clients who … and it's not easy … but having people come to me who want that thing. And I am going to work very hard to maintain that. I know that I have a signature in the work, and it's actually something I fight against all the time. But the way I do it is I keep low overhead and I am a small studio and I live a very simple life.

When you make a sticker that says, "Advertisers think you're stupid," do you worry no advertising agency will ever hire you? Or do you think, "I don't care. I don't want to work for an advertising agency."

Yeah, but how can you live like that? Living in fear. I have always felt that the right people will find me. And I think only stupid advertisers are insulted by that. The people that it's meant to turn off. And you know what? I am dealing with this thing now where I would rather die with the reputation that I have than with fifty dollars more in my pocket. If some agency doesn't want to work with me because I have insulted them, then they're pussies and I don't want to work with them to begin with.

How often are you able to combine the work you're doing for love and the work you're doing for money?

In my book [*Victore or, Who Died and Made You Boss?*], I talk about this. I believe there are some jobs you do for God and some jobs you do for money, and I approach every job as a God job. I approach every job as something I want to make awesome, but if something happens along the way and it turns into a money job, then we just get it done and get paid.

Why is self-directed work important to you? And do you think it's going to become a revenue stream that supports you?

We will see if it becomes a revenue stream, as they say. Part of it is because of a level of disillusionment with the commercial jobs that are out there. Rarely when I talk to a client do I feel like they're committed and they actually want good work instead of stuff that looks like everything else. So there's a level of disillusionment. I know that people like my work, and I am trying to figure out how to basically get it straight to them without the middleman.
I did a talk in New York just a couple of weeks ago and it was called "86 The Middleman," and it's about how to do this thing, how to get rid of those pesky clients.

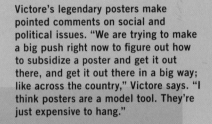

Victore's legendary posters make pointed comments on social and political issues. "We are trying to make a big push right now to figure out how to subsidize a poster and get it out there, and get it out there in a big way; like across the country," Victore says. "I think posters are a model tool. They're just expensive to hang."

*Would you say that's your goal? To get rid
of the pesky clients? Make money selling
your own work?*

Yes. There are some clients that I will
always work for. I am starting a big
venture with Esquire magazine. They are
[a company] that I believe in and I have
worked with before and enjoyed, and there
are a few other clients that we have that I
will always work for, but mostly I am trying
to work on other surfaces and try other
things and still have a voice and still have
a signature.

*A lot of young designers want to do work
they feel is meaningful and that makes a
difference. What would you say to them?*

Oh, I tell them go for it. Go for it. Two
things that go well together are ambition
and ignorance.

You know, go for it before you have
bills and go for it before people start
disillusioning you and before the naysayers
start coming out.

www.jamesvictore.com

Want to own a piece of
Victore? He now sells one-of-
a-kind hand-painted bottles
on Etsy. It's part of his effort
to cut out the middleman and
deliver his work directly.

NEXT STEPS

What project idea(s) have you been kicking around in your head?

Do you know anyone who might want to partner with you?

Or anyone who could give you advice?

Do you need funding?

☐ Yes   ☐ No

If yes, how much would get you started?

$

Which of these funding sources might work for you?

☐ Self-funding
☐ Donations
☐ Grants
☐ Investors
☐ Sponsorships
☐ Crowd funding: Kickstarter (www.kickstarter.com)
  or IndieGoGo (www.indiegogo.com)

How soon can you start working on your own project? (We vote for today!)

NEED AN EXTRA DOSE OF MOXIE TO GET YOU STARTED?
For extra-credit homework, we implore you to find and read Tibor Kalman's essay, "Fuck Committees (I Believe in Lunatics)," about the difficulty of doing meaningful personal work in a bland corporate culture. Kalman is a great example of working both sides of the fence: Using corporate money to do good things. If you the essay hooks you, there's a great survey of his work and life in *Tibor Kalman, Perverse Optimist* edited by Peter Hall and Michael Bierut.

etro **QUARTERLY**

SPRING 2007

Planning for the New

Metro **QUARTE**

Metro Means Business

Metro's partnership with business keeps
LA County moving forward.

$90 million annual purchases

Metro **QUARTERLY**

WINTER/SPRING 2008

Choosing a Transit Future
Imagine the possibilities.

Metro **QUARTE**

FALL 2007

SUMMER 2008

4. WORKING ON THE INSIDE

Think of socially conscious design as a process rather than something you have to hit square on the nose. Designers at Metro Los Angeles made Metro Quarterly more environmentally friendly over time, using recycled paper then ultimately producing an FSC-certified issue. A sustainability message on the back made this clear to readers.

We don't think being an activist means you have to quit your day job. In fact, a corporate environment or a traditional agency puts you in the thick of things and allows you to work inside the system to create meaningful change. If you have a design gig at a giant company (or such companies are your clients), even small improvements add up fast across a large brand. You might be part of an industry that desperately needs change or perhaps you've landed an in-house job that's already committed to social change.

That said, this was the toughest chapter of the book to write. From our original call for submissions, we received only one entry from an in-house design department. Some PR departments weren't too keen on letting their employees talk to us when they heard it was for a book with the word *activist* in the title. This was true even though we approached those teams because they were doing work we wanted to celebrate. We suspect it's tough to go on the record about ethical dilemmas and tough decisions if you work for a big corporation and want to keep your job.

Ultimately, we think this is an area where a lot of great stuff is already happening, with the opportunity for even more. A lot of design walks hand in hand with commerce, and this close relationship means that designers directly influence how business works. This chapter covers strategies for encouraging and carrying out positive change in the capacity of in-house designer—all without losing your job.

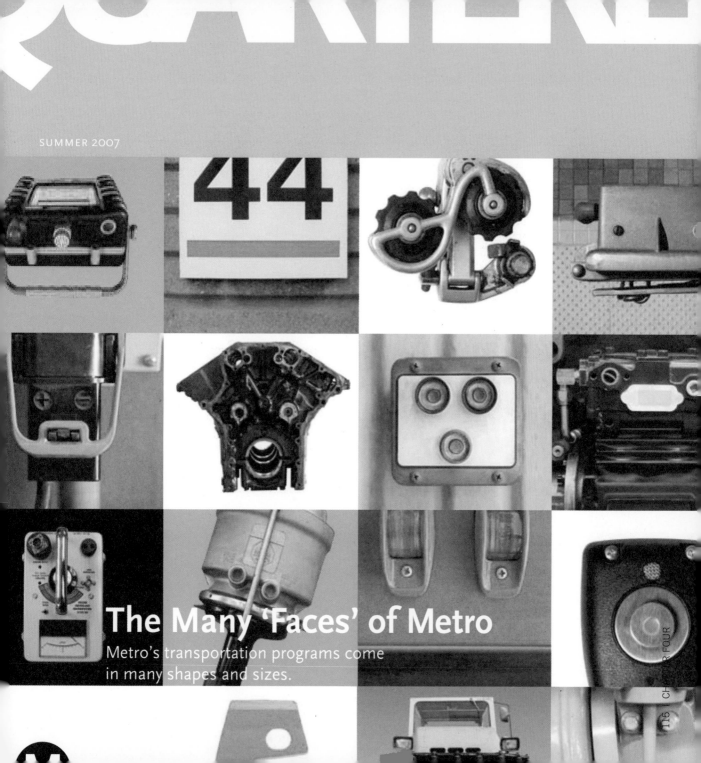

SUMMER 2007

44

The Many 'Faces' of Metro

Metro's transportation programs come
in many shapes and sizes.

Not every change takes: Senior designer Michele Moore switched the Metro Los Angeles Works mailer from coated stock to uncoated recycled paper. But the new stock soaked up too much ink, and ultimately, the publication went back to the original paper.

BEING THE (POLITELY) SQUEAKY WHEEL

As a senior designer at Metro Los Angeles, Michele Moore spends her time designing projects that promote public transportation in one way or another. Social responsibility is baked into her job, but as she knows, there's always room for improvement. In fact, you might say Moore is on a personal mission to get more of Metro's projects printed on recycled and/or Forest Stewardship Council (FSC) certified paper (see sidebar on page 119). And she's not afraid to lobby for these more environmentally friendly options with internal clients and peers. "I have certainly earned my fair share of eye rolls," she says, laughing. "People are just sick of hearing it from me."

This Metro Los Angeles bike map is FSC certified and helps people get around the city in a more sustainable manner.

Moore's interest in FSC happened almost by accident when she wanted to print a project on recycled paper to promote Metro's interest in sustainability. Unfortunately, the paper she needed didn't come in a recycled version, but as her printer pointed out, it was FSC certified. "She explained the whole thing to me and I thought, how am I ever going to take this back to the office and explain it?" Moore says. Luckily, the printer offered to put together and conduct a seminar for the Metro's marketing and design staff, which explained what FSC is, how to use the logo and any other questions that came up.

FSC PAPER EXPLAINED

A lot of people talk about FSC certified paper, but not all of them understand what it means. FSC stands for Forest Stewardship Council. It's an independent third-party organization that certifies papers that come from a forest that's managed to meet an extensive set of environmental and social standards.

There's also a chain-of-custody aspect to the certification that tracks paper from the forest to the mill, merchant and printer. This ensures you that your paper really comes from where you think it does. It's also the reason you have to print your project at an FSC certified printer in order to use the logo. Learn more at www.fsc.org or talk with a certified printer.

REDUCE REUSE RECYCLE

Metro Los Angeles designers created this bright, playful poster for the Metro Cafe, the on-site cafeteria, to encourage recycling at the office.

Let energy conservation begin with your workstation. Turn off your computer and the light under your overhead cabinet when you leave for the day.

Metro

These days Moore is known as something of an FSC expert in the office, and her boss might even email and ask her for a blurb to explain FSC. But she's met her share of resistance and failure as she works toward greener choices, too. Sometimes budgets, schedules and other issues get in the way of going with FSC or recycled papers, and when that happens, Moore accepts the situation and moves on. (The materials don't generally cost more than traditional ones, but FSC printers can be higher in price—as well as quality). For one Metro publication, Moore made the switch to an uncoated recycled paper and the sheet soaked up a lot of ink. Readers missed the bright colors. For the next issue, they went back to the original coated stock.

Whether you're interested in greener paper or another issue entirely, Moore's story is a great example of how to position yourself as a resource within the office and to use your voice to push for slow and steady change. She's introduced a number of people to FSC from scratch, explaining how it can improve a client's image and impact the greater good at the same time. Her best advice for other in-house designers? "Keep at it because the more of an example you can be, the more people will notice," she says.

Metro Store: Green Shirt

Details:
> artwork size 4.75 x 3.25"
> 2.5" down from neck
> prints 1-color, white
> centered left to right on shirt

Actual Size

I ride for a
greener LA.
Ⓜ Metro

3.25 in.

4.75 in.

2.5 in.

I ride for a
greener LA.
Ⓜ Metro

Front

Both the message and the material for this Metro Los Angeles T-shirt are green. The shirts are made with unbleached organic cotton and natural dyes.

One space, many faces: This 2,500-square-foot exhibition space at the Liberty Science Center changes twice a year, which is why it was designed to reuse as many materials as possible. For starters, it boasts a modular structure with aluminum overhead trusses, cabinets, shelving and interpretive framework. The components are mobile, allowing for a rearrangement of the physical space. When paired with a graphic skin, these modular pieces create a distinct look and feel for a variety of exhibit topics, as shown.

DEVELOPING GUIDELINES OR BEST PRACTICES

Want another way to encourage positive change at your in-house design group? Think about how you'll approach environmental and social issues as a whole instead of addressing them as they come up. At the Liberty Science Center in Jersey City, New Jersey, it makes sense for the in-house design department to have a brief document (about three pages) that outlines its overall approach to sustainable exhibit design. After all, part of the center's stated mission is to "strengthen communities and advance global stewardship."

The top-level guidelines outline a series of ten strategies and best practices including: support local suppliers, consider multifunctionalism, reduce consumables and design for longevity. It also outlines specific ideas and choices for making just about every stage of the design process more environmentally friendly. Some of these are fairly obvious (use biodegradable inks) while others require designers to dig deeper (establish criteria for end-of-life processing). A lot of the value lies in having these goals and considerations listed in one place. It's a helpful reminder of what you're working toward, along with some ideas on how you might get there.

The main front entry wall and lobby of Liberty Science Center were designed with glass panels to produce a dramatic architectural effect using natural light. The fritted architectural glass and mural images help keep the building cool and reduce pressure on the air conditioning.

While the guidelines offer things to consider rather than mandates, it's clear that the in-house design team at Liberty Science Center takes sustainability seriously. They've created a modular framework system for an exhibit space that changes every six months, so they can rearrange and re-skin it to create a new experience with fewer materials. Plus, they're always considering what might be a better material or process, such as using mechanical fasteners instead of adhesives. "I think there's a lot of information out there," says Ann Neumann, director of design and new media. "You don't have to create everything from scratch." This is especially true for those who do the homework in advance and create a cheat sheet with their own set of guidelines.

HOW TO BE AN ACTIVIST WITHOUT GETTING FIRED

If you're working in a traditional corporate environment, it can be tricky to bill yourself as an activist without putting your job in jeopardy. How can you lobby for change without pissing off your boss and co-workers, and still fulfill the core duties of your job?

Here are some tips for gently rocking the boat without getting tossed overboard.

Make the business case. If your company isn't very progressive, frame your case in terms of what they do care about. Will using less material for the annual report save money? Is being involved with local charities a good way to bolster the company's reputation? Target your message to the audience.

Position yourself as a resource. No one likes a complainer. Instead, set yourself up as the go-to person for social and environmental issues. Share case studies, research and success stories with colleagues. Be the person in the office who can explain the benefits of soy inks. Know how and why consumers respond to companies who do social and environmental good.

Pace yourself and set realistic goals. Your employer isn't going to change the way he or she works overnight. Take an honest look at your environment and start off with a few attainable goals. Celebrate small victories.

Avoid ultimatums and sanctimony. Design activism isn't going to seem very sexy if you're constantly judging your co-workers and company. Instead, remember that you're all on the same team and approach this process collaboratively. Look for places where the company mission overlaps with your activist interests.

Create a tribe within the tribe. You're going to need some co-conspirators to start a movement. Look for like-minded folks throughout the company and figure out ways to work together.

AN ACTIVIST
ON STAFF

BY NOAH SCALIN

Before I started my own company, I spent six years running the in-house design departments for two different businesses in New York City. Neither specialized in social causes or environmental issues, but I was still able to get them to make some choices about their business practices based on my own convictions.

The first thing I realized is that while a business might not be overtly interested in the issues, usually the individuals who work there care on a personal level. It's much easier to talk to people one-on-one about breathing clean air and drinking clean water than it is to discuss the CO_2 emissions of a factory with your boss. If we started from a place of agreement on some basic issues, it was easier to talk casually about how the company might work on those issues, too.

As a designer, I was an individual cog in a much larger machine, but I still had the opportunity to choose which direction to turn or to decide not to turn at all. Granted, I couldn't throw a monkey wrench into the gears anytime I wanted and still keep my job. Instead, I used every decision-making opportunity to offer alternative solutions to things I thought were socially or environmentally harmful. Not all my ideas saw light, but I was always given the chance to air my concerns, because it was in an area in which I was considered the expert.

The key to getting my ideas pushed through was to use the language of business. And since this was before anyone knew the phrase "corporate social responsibility," I had to talk about money. Luckily, doing the right thing often reduces budgets because it usually leads to less waste, more loyal customers and even more efficient employees.

When I was working for a fashion company, one of my assignments was to design a shopping bag for their stores. They had been using cheap disposable plastic bags. I suggested a switch to heavy-duty paper bags with nice printing and rope handles. In other words, something people would want to actually carry around more than once. This was before the prevalence of cloth shopping bags, but the company still went for it. The stores even used less bags overall because the cashiers who filled them viewed the new bags as more precious objects.

Some of what I did was under the radar (ordering eco-friendly office supplies whenever I was given a chance), but I was also up-front about my beliefs from the start. By engaging my bosses in what mattered to me right away, I began a dialogue that allowed me to bring things up later that I might have felt uncomfortable saying out of the blue. In the end, it was about making incremental changes towards a larger goal and keeping in mind that some change is better than none at all.

CHANGING THE OFFICE

In-house designers can have a positive influence beyond the projects they do for their clients and the public in general. There's also all the day-to-day happenings inside the office. Are you and your fellow designers operating in a sustainable and ethical way on a day-to-day basis? You probably have some influence on everything from recycling office paper to choosing vendors who operate in an ethical manner. Survey your day-to-day work environment for ways to have an impact. At the Metro Los Angeles in-house design department, for instance, they take the single-sided prints from the color printer and turn them into little notebooks that utilize the blank side.

Senior designer Mark Boediaman designed these posters, which were hung around the Clif Bar offices to inspire employees to make sustainable choices.

WASH YOUR HANDS OF WATER WASTE.

ON AVERAGE, WASHING DISHES BY HAND USES ABOUT 20 GALLONS OF WATER. Energy Star dishwashers only use about 4 gallons of water per load, and even standard machines use less, at around 6 gallons.

BONUS FACT: An energy smart washer can save more water in one year than one person drinks in an entire lifetime!

BUBBLE BUBBLE TOILET IN TROUBLE…

THE AVERAGE TOILET USES 3.5-7 GALLONS PER FLUSH (or 1.6 gallons with a water saving toilet), so only flush what you must. Tissue, insects (that you absolutely couldn't spare), and anything you're trying to hide from the police should be thrown in the wastebasket.

BONUS FACT: An elephant can smell water up to 3 miles away.

UNSCREW A LIGHT BULB. DO THE SAME FOR THE PLANET.

Only about 10 percent of the energy used by an incandescent bulb creates light. The rest of the bulb only creates heat. Wait!?!?

SWAP THOSE OLD BULBS OUT FOR NEWER, COOLER, MORE EFFICIENT, 10x LONGER LASTING CFL BULBS.

BONUS FACT: Recycling one glass bottle saves enough energy to light a 100-watt bulb for four hours.

THE SATURDAY EVENING COMPOST.

FOOD AND PAPER ARE THE TWO LARGEST CONTRIBUTORS to landfill, and make up more than half of all landfill waste — more than all plastics, diapers, Styrofoam, and tires, COMBINED.

BONUS FACT: Berkeley collects commercial food scraps to produce a high quality compost used in community and urban gardens.

NOT ALL PAPER CUTS ARE BAD.

IN A RECENT TRASH SORT, 85% OF THE PAPER THAT WAS DISCARDED HAD A CLEAN SIDE TO IT! Help cut down on paper waste by printing only what you must, printing double-sided whenever possible, and recycling EVERYTHING left over.

BONUS FACT: 1 ton (2,240 pounds) of office paper = 24 trees!

HOW LOW CAN YOU FLOW?

A SHOWER WITH A LOW-FLOW SHOWERHEAD OUTPUTS AN AVERAGE OF 9-12 GALLONS PER PERSON, PER DAY. High-flow showerheads are even worse! So keep those showers short. Ideally, no longer than 5 minutes.

BONUS FACT: Cutting one minute off your shower time can save about 200 gallons of water per month.

ARE YOU GREENWASHING?

If you're not familiar with the term, greenwashing is when companies make themselves or their products seem more environmentally friendly than they actually are. In a 2010 study conducted TerraChoice Environmental Marketing, Inc., more than 95 percent of the consumer products examined were found guilty of this advertising sin. Learn more about the study and how you can avoid the sins of greenwashing at: **http://sinsofgreenwashing.org**

At Clif Bar, senior designer Mark Boediman designed a series of posters to promote sustainability and individual accountability within the office, helping to reduce the company's footprint. The posters serve as daily encouragement for employees to do things like conserve water and make the most use of paper. The bright colors and clever headlines give the posters a fun and inspirational tone that makes you want to lighten your ecological impact.

In reality, almost anything that helps people in any way falls under the broad umbrella of socially conscious design. The in-house design team at Merck actually expanded its role to help improve the look, feel and function of interior spaces. "We want to make sure that when people are in the office they're in a space that's stimulating," say Bob Calvano, director of media services. They've introduced bright colors and graphics to the office to create dynamic spaces that encourage collaboration.

How can your department move beyond its traditional boundaries to make a difference? "Get in front of the right people and pitch ideas," Calvano says. "This stuff is going to start with some initiative on your part."

The in-house design team at Merck introduced bright graphics into the office with photomicrographs of chemical compounds—an appropriate choice for a drug company geared toward making its office spaces more lively and inviting for employees.

DESIGN REBEL:

Elan Cole: Asking the Right Questions

IN THE DAVID AND GOLIATH METAPHOR, JOHNSON & JOHNSON IS DEFINITELY GOLIATH. But who says a giant can't use its size for good? Before coming to Johnson & Johnson, Elan Cole didn't have much training in sustainability, but now it's part of the global creative director's daily work life. The idea of sustainable design is built into the way his team—and the company's entire Global Strategic Design Office (GSDO)—approaches every project. "For the designers, it's really about how little material and how little impact can we have?" he says.

The company's design office continually strives to lessen its environmental footprint, and as an illustrated reminder, they have even hung an image showing a Johnson & Johnson baby bottle in a dump. It's true that big companies might not be able to change as quickly and nimbly as small ones, but they do have more resources and the power of scale on their side. The GSDO, for instance, includes an engineering department that helps ensure

> **"ALL YOU HAVE TO DO IS START ASKING YOURSELF, 'WHAT WOULD HAPPEN IF THIS ENDED UP IN A PARK RIGHT UP THE STREET? WHAT WOULD HAPPEN IF A MILLION OF THESE THINGS GET SHIPPED TO THE DUMP?'"**

the company's packaging materials and manufacturing procedures are as sustainable as they can be.

In the following interview, Cole describes what else goes on behind the scenes at this environmentally minded in-house design department.

What kind of sustainability questions does your team ask when working on a project?

The questions are inspired by Chris Hacker, our chief design officer. One is, whenever you get a design brief, ask yourself, "Does it need to be done?" That is probably the most rhetorical question. If you're getting a project, you're probably not going to say, "'I don't think this needs to be done." But it challenges you to think about the true necessity.

The second question is sort of drilling down from the macro. Does this element need to be here? Does this package need to be this big? How is it actually packed to the shipper? Does the material need to be this material? Does it need to be this many? Does it need to be this much? Does the ink need to be this?

In an overhaul of the Listerine® packaging, the team at Johnson & Johnson reduced the thickness of the plastic bottle by 30 percent. Doing so saved materials and money, as well as cut down on shipping weight.

Anything else you think is important to ask?
You know, the flip side of it is asking the question that every designer is trained to ask, which is, "What can it be? What should it be?" In that sense, I think designers are trained from the get-go.

All you have to do is start asking yourself, "What would happen if this ended up in a park right up the street? What would happen if a million of these things get shipped to the dump?" I think when you start to contextualize the work that we do, it will help you guide your decision in a more reflexive and fundamental way.

Can you tell me about a success story? Something Johnson & Johnson redesigned that made a positive impact?
We did a project for Band-Aid inspired by the tin boxes that Band-Aids used to come in. It was a project that we did for Costco. Normally, the approach was large bulk packaging. There really wasn't much there for the consumer besides a gigantic box filled with Band-Aids.

What we did was create a system of interlocking pods that actually could be detached from each other and placed in different areas; placed in the car, placed in the office, placed in the home. Long after the Band-Aids are used, you can either fill

the pod with more bandages or fill it up with other things and use it for storage, which a lot of people are still doing.

Any other inspiring projects?
On the materials side, we have a major plant in Brazil, and all of the cardboard material that is made there is actually farmed from a fast-growing eucalyptus forest. It is a cultivated forest.

The trees are actually engineered to grow significantly faster. You raise a crop of trees, you have another plot that's raising the next crop of trees, another plot that's raising the next crop of trees after that, and you essentially have a natural production line of raw material.

The trees are harvested, pulp and paper made, and then it's a renewable resource. The farming is extremely well managed by local people.

What's it like to work on greener packaging efforts at such a big corporation?
For a company like J&J, it's a much longer journey and a much bigger boat to turn than a small business. We look at a product like Listerine, and it's a very difficult product from a sustainability standpoint. It's a big plastic bottle with a lot of liquid. It's heavy when you ship it.

We ended up reducing the wall thickness of the bottle by 30 percent. We saved a number of tons of plastic and a number of millions of dollars on the overall materials cost. From a sustainability standpoint, it's not the sexiest of stories. But I think what it does illustrate is that you have to start somewhere.

For me, the learning curve, it's kind of like going on a diet in a way. A lot of people that go on a diet are like, "Damn it, I didn't lose 40 pounds in the first week," and then they go back and eat ice cream every day. You know, this journey has to start with a learning curve. It has to start with education. It has to start with small steps.

If you can reduce 30 percent of the plastic in the production of millions of bottles of Listerine, yes, it's still a plastic, but it's only 70 percent of what you've been doing.

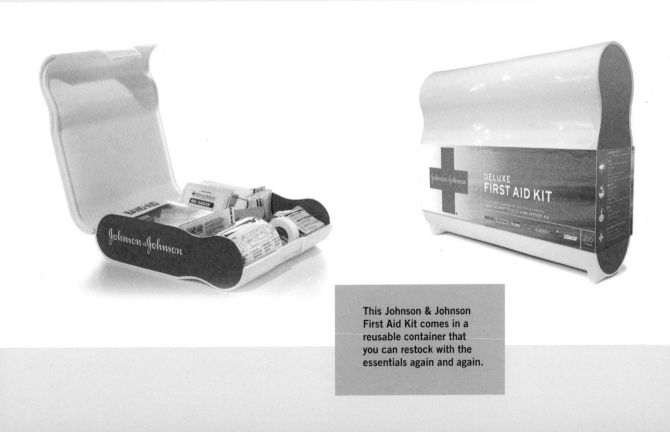

This Johnson & Johnson First Aid Kit comes in a reusable container that you can restock with the essentials again and again.

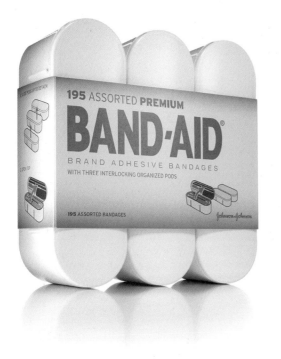

Maybe you change the plastic next. Then maybe you change the printing method and the shipping method.

What advice would you give in-house designers working at corporations that aren't focused on sustainability and other socially conscious design issues? How can they help plant some seeds?
I think designers at times forget that they are designers when it comes to certain things. As a designer, our job is to solve problems. Our job is to say, "Here's the problem, what are the causes of this

problem? What are the ways that I can approach it? How do I want to tackle it? What are my goals? What are my agendas? What are the five different approaches I can take? What's the best approach given the circumstances?"

I think finding your allies is important, seeing if it's happening in other places in the company, treating it like a defined problem and being realistic about what can be achieved in six months. What can I achieve in a year? What can I achieve in two years? Where do I want to go with this? How far can I take this with this company?

Then I think not being afraid to make mistakes and absolutely understanding that you have to learn from them are imperative. Also, understanding that it takes small steps to do big things. I don't want to sound like a fortune cookie, but it's true.

What would you say to people who believe big companies are the problem and can't really be a meaningful part of the solution?
I had never worked for a big company before Johnson & Johnson. Before this, I was design director at The Museum of Modern Art. But now I think my role as an activist is to get more people to work for corporations in a design role and to change them from within.

Over the past five years, we have developed unprecedented partnerships within the company so that we're co-owners of the result, and that didn't happen overnight. It happened because of us going deeper and deeper into the processes, into the creative development of the brand, the equity. You know, you find that if you want to change something, changing from within is sometimes the most impact that you can have.

NEXT STEPS

What change(s) would you like to see at your place of work?

How realistic do you think those are?

Which small piece would be easiest to tackle first?

Think of three co-workers who might want to be involved:

1.

2.

3.

Does your team have guidelines for sustainability?

☐ Yes   ☐ No

If not, have you thought about working with your boss on a side project that develops some?

5. YOUR PLAN OF ACTION

Studio Sonda in Croatia took the leftover posters from the 2008 BOOKtiga used book festival and painted over them to create the 2009 posters. In addition to reusing goods, the project actually celebrates used goods as something with equal value to new items.

We hope that what you have read so far about all of the inspiring design rebels out in the world has you fired up. It is possible to make a living and make a difference at the same time. But so many times there's this wide gap between ideas and action. It can feel like you have to leap over the Grand Canyon—alone, in a single bound—to turn your hopes and dreams into reality. That's where this chapter comes into play. We want to give you some concrete next steps to turn your excitement and passion into meaningful action.

6 IDEAS
TO GET YOU STARTED

You can't do everything all at once, but we wanted to give you some prompts you can start working on tomorrow (or today if it's early enough in the morning). A little action often spurs a lot of momentum. The key is to just get started. And remember, we're cheering for you.

JOIN THE MOVEMENT

You're not alone as a design activist. The AIGA has created an initiative called Design for Good to help you make a social impact with your talent and skills. Check out all the tools, resources and inspiration right here: **www.aiga.org/design-for-good.**

CHAPTER FIVE

1.
FUND ONE OF YOUR IDEAS
WITH KICKSTARTER OR INDIEGOGO

Money always seems to be a big barrier to getting your own projects out into the world but with the websites Kickstarter (www.kickstarter.com) and IndieGoGo (www.indiegogo.com), it's easier than ever to get money for your project. Nathan Wessel played around with simplifying the complicated Cincinnati bus route maps after reading a blog post about transit frequency maps. Soon the activist and urban-planning student realized his simplified map could encourage more people to take public transportation. He wanted to see more people getting out of their cars and interacting with each other in more meaningful ways.

Several people suggested he try using Kickstarter to raise funds to print his map. Despite a lack of interest in his project from the transit authority, he went ahead on his own, creating a video and putting the project on the crowd-funding site. What's the key to making it work? "You can't just put it out there and wait for everybody to donate," he says. "Ask people directly, and ask hard. 'Okay, fifty dollars from you, how about that?'" After appearing on a few blogs and in the local paper, word about his project spread through social media. Kickstarter funded an initial print run of the maps, and the student government at the University of Cincinnati hopes to print maps and give them out to freshmen.

STEAL THIS DESIGN

When you're a design a rebel, traditional copyright law doesn't always meet your needs. You might want other activists to be able to download and print your protest posters. Or maybe you're working on an open-source project that encourages people to build on your initial work. Then again, maybe you just want people to freely access and share your designs online. What's a design rebel to do? Consider applying one of the Creative Commons copyright licenses to your work. They allow you to grant different levels of acceptable sharing and use. Find all the details at: **http://creativecommons.org.**

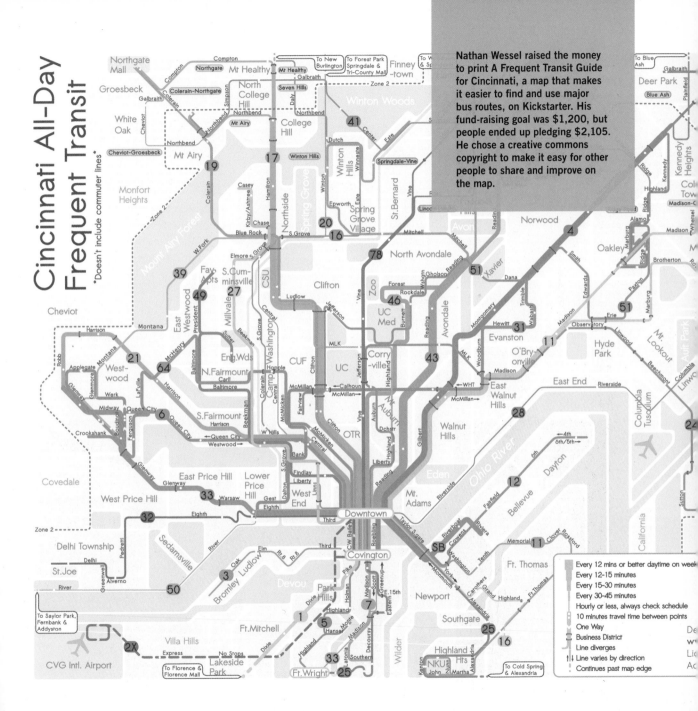

Nathan Wessel raised the money to print A Frequent Transit Guide for Cincinnati, a map that makes it easier to find and use major bus routes, on Kickstarter. His fund-raising goal was $1,200, but people ended up pledging $2,105. He chose a creative commons copyright to make it easy for other people to share and improve on the map.

2.

FIND SOME CO-CONSPIRATORS
AND A CAUSE YOU CARE ABOUT

We think social movements work best when lots of folks get involved, so give yourself a boost by finding some fellow designers interested in similar issues. Then put your heads together to figure out how you can all make a difference. The members of Justseeds, an artists' cooperative with members in fourteen cities and three countries, have created a series of socially or politically engaged art portfolios together. The images in each portfolio revolve around a different theme, and they're created in partnership with a group or series of groups already working on the issue.

Justseeds teamed up with Iraq Veterans Against the War to address the issue of traumatized soldiers being sent back to the Middle East. Other portfolios have focused on prison justice

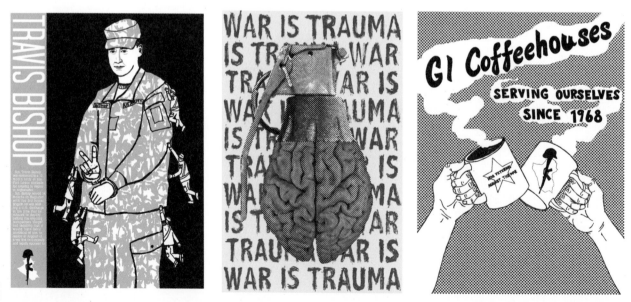

Members of the artists' cooperative Justseeds work together to create image portfolios for social or political organizations working on causes the artists care about. These posters were created in partnership with Iraq Veterans Against the War. They were pasted up in Chicago and even used on military bases in training. From left to right, artwork by Alec Dunn, Jesse Purcell, Molly Fair, Pete Yahnke, Tom Cilvil and Josh MacPhee.

and environmental issues. The resulting work often ends up as printed pieces, which can be sold to raise money for each cause. High-res digital versions are made available for other groups to use in their activism and organizing for free. You might even see these creations hanging up on a street corner or in an exhibit.

"One of the things that can make a portfolio powerful is that it's not a single voice," says Josh MacPhee, a member of Justseeds. "It's polyvocal and everyone is bringing their own voice and æsthetic to it. It's that multiplicity of voices that can amplify the larger vision or the larger voice." This wide range of styles and approaches also gives viewers more opportunity to make a true connection with one of the images.

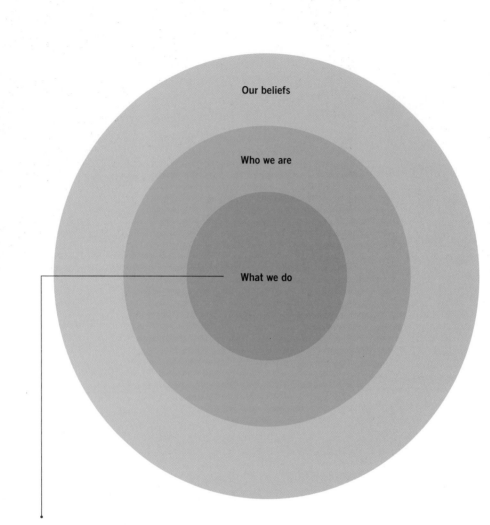

Our beliefs

Who we are

What we do

Thinkers
"Defining the problem is 99% of the
solution." This age-old saying sums up
our approach to design. We engage our
clients in conversations that define an
approach for their long-term needs, not
just the best solution for now.

3.

DIAGRAM THE WAY YOU WANT TO WORK

Design is a visual medium, so it only makes sense to diagram the way your beliefs and ethics will interact with your professional life. At MSLK, a boutique marketing and design agency in New York, the team put themselves through the same branding and marketing exercise they put clients through to help define their business. "We had to apply it to ourselves," says Marc S. Levitt, cofounder and creative director. "It took longer. But it's very worth it."

One of the results of that internal exercise was this diagram the firm refers to as "the jawbreaker." It shows how MSLK's beliefs, including a strong environmental bent, encompass everything else they do. How does this apply to you? Why not take the time to define your beliefs, professional identity and area of focus by making your own jawbreaker? Or find another way to visually marry your job and ethics—maybe a Venn diagram, pie chart, flowchart or series of photos.

MSLK created this jawbreaker diagram to clearly define the focus of their business, which has a strong sustainability thread. "Clients say, 'Well, my company is not that green. So, I don't know why I would even bother doing this one piece green,'" says Levitt. "We say, 'It's fine. Every little bit counts.' I think we try to poke holes in the myth that you have to be squeaky green to have anything make a difference."

I ♥ NY

4.

START DOING THE KIND OF WORK YOU WISH PEOPLE WOULD PAY YOU FOR

There's probably some kind of design project you've been wishing someone would hire you to do. Maybe it's protest signs, political posters or just an educational brochure. But you know what? You don't have to wait for someone else to fund your idea. "People can try to find the funds or people can fund themselves," says John Emerson, a designer, writer and activist in New York. "Every time I have initiated a project of my own, whether it's a poster or a T-shirt or a website, the effort has always come back to me in some kind of unexpected way."

Just one example: To protest the Republican National Convention in New York, Emerson replaced the heart in the famous "I heart NY" logo with an upside down elephant, the Republican party logo. Then he took the image to several nonprofit groups. Unfortunately, they couldn't use the image because it was too political. But one of the groups, United for Peace and Justice, tapped Emerson months later when they needed posters and fliers to publicize events and hand out at the events themselves. Emerson also turned that original image into T-shirts and sold a few on his own.

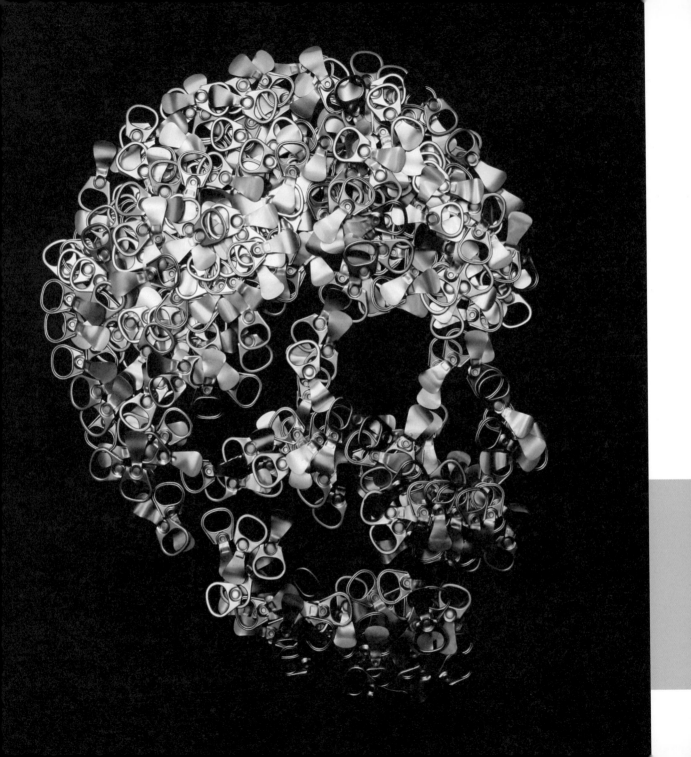

5.

MAKE A DAILY COMMITMENT TO DOING SOMETHING DIFFERENT

Sometimes doing what you love is better than doing what you think you should to move farther along your path. When my coauthor, Noah, was looking for a creative outlet separate from client work, he came up with the idea to do a daily online art project called "Skull-A-Day." He literally made one skull every day for a year. The project required him to carve out a little time each day for this fun, personal work. When he first started, he didn't realize the energy and time spent would add up to so much more than the individual pieces of art.

Noah stuck with it for 365 days, and in the process the project racked up tens of thousands of fans around the world, a Webby award, a book deal and even an appearance on *The Martha Stewart Show*. How did it help his design career? The project introduced countless people to Noah's work, and he ended up with a body of art he could license and exhibit, as well as new skills to apply to client work. Skull-A-Day also launched a series of creativity talks that Noah has delivered to everyone from New York City high school students to designers at the CIA.

Not only did Noah's art inspire marines in Iraq to make their own creative work, but they inspired Noah, too. A care package sent from the USMC Skulz (a marine unit) included a bag full of old-fashioned soda can pull-tabs, which Noah made into a skull even though his project officially ended nearly a year before.

Starting to wonder what this has to do with socially conscious design? The Skull-A-Day site lives on as a creative community that encourages other people to pursue creative projects. It has inspired everyone from art teachers in China and the UK to marines based in Iraq. There's even a group of librarians that use the book that resulted from this project as a way to encourage reading among teens. These are people Noah would have never reached had he pursued change through only the usual paths. Just think what spending time on your own personal projects might achieve.

6.

CHALLENGE YOURSELF
TO CELEBRATE USED MATERIALS

In U.S. consumer culture, we're constantly being sold on the value of shiny new stuff. It's a message ever present on TV commercials, billboards, banner ads and packaging. What if you decided to turn that notion on its head? What if you made it a point to celebrate used materials? This notion takes reuse and recycling one step farther.

In Croatia, Studio Sonda took the leftover posters from the 2008 BOOKtiga used-book festival and hand-painted over them for the 2009 festival. They wanted to send a message: Used goods, cleverly employed, can have the same value as new ones. There's a charm to these posters that a slick offset piece would have a hard time reproducing. And it's a reminder of all the possibilities available to you when you work with resources that already exist.

Don't be afraid to get your hands dirty. Studio Sonda in Croatia painted over old posters to make new ones for a used-book festival. It's more interesting, thoughtful and clever than something new.

THE DESIGN REBEL
WORK SHEET:
HOW TO GET THERE
FROM HERE

Which working methods appeal to you most? (check as many as apply)

☐ Starting a socially conscious design business
☐ Working for a socially conscious business
☐ Pursuing self-directed side projects
☐ Working for change from the inside (i.e., a corporate job)
☐ Founding a nonprofit
☐ Giving a grant of your services
☐ Creating and selling your own socially responsible products

Is there a designer or firm's story in this book that inspired you most? Who was it and why?

What issues are nearest and dearest to your heart? (check as many as apply)

☐ the environment
☐ workers' rights
☐ women's issues
☐ LGBTQ issues
☐ public transportation
☐ bicycling
☐ consumerism
☐ peace
☐ poverty
☐ education

☐ Other:

☐ Other:

☐ Other:

☐ Other:

☐ Other:

☐ Other:

List and describe three ideas for design rebel projects you've had in the past but never started:

1.

2.

3.

You're passionate and creative. So what's stopping you from pursuing these projects and passions? (check all that apply)

☐ Fear
☐ Lack of funds
☐ Lack of time
☐ Lack of knowledge
☐ Lack of co-conspirators
☐ Not sure where and how to start
☐ Don't think it will make a difference
☐ Other

What are five practical things you can do to start working around these blocks?

1.

2.

3.

4.

5.

How will you feel if you start changing your career today into the one you dream about?

How will you feel in six months or a year if you keep doing what you're doing now?

What's the worst thing that could happen if you start reimagining your career? And how likely is that outcome to happen?

What's the best thing that could happen if you start reimagining your career into one that aligns with your values and beliefs?

DESIGN REBEL:

Ennis Carter: Mission Possible

WAY BACK IN 1996, BEFORE EVERYONE WAS TALKING ABOUT SOCIALLY CONSCIOUS DESIGN, Ennis Carter launched a business called Design for Social Impact (now called Social Impact Studios). Armed with her background as an organizer, she set up shop in the corner of her Philadelphia bedroom and started bringing her design and storytelling savvy to the nonprofit world.

Today she has a studio, a staff and a client list that includes roughly six hundred groups. The firm does everything from design and identity work to strategic planning and organizational power mapping. A simple mission is the driving force behind it all: Combine artistry and activism to call attention to important social issues.

"WHEN YOU BELIEVE IN WHAT YOU'RE DOING, YOU CAN DO ANYTHING WHETHER OR NOT YOU HAVE THE RESOURCES OR THE CAPACITY OR ALL THE SKILLS."

A lot of designers would like to do more meaningful work. Any advice?

I would say that you can project beautiful, meaningful and thoughtful work in anything you do. Honestly, I'm not offended by the fact that the corporate world has caught up with our idea of selling happiness. I don't know if you've noticed but all of a sudden it's like everybody's selling happiness. Like Pepsi and Coke are selling happiness, and the slogan for Honey Nut Cheerios is "Bee happy. Bee healthy." Everybody is talking about health and happiness. I take that as a victory, that we have gotten a message out there that is the key aspiration.

I actually think it's good for people to not just abandon the corporate world but to actually be in it and to express themselves and bring their values to work. But then if they want to do some other things that are related to social impact, they should find something they care deeply about and do design work around that. It might mean working for very low prices or for free, but it is really going to give you an opportunity for what I call soul work. I think it's a matter of committing to it and seeing where it takes you. I think the difference is not being afraid.

What do you mean by "not being afraid"?

I think our culture tells us a lot of things. The average person in our country doesn't make as much money as what we're told we should be making. So there's a fear of not succeeding and not being able to buy a house or live where you want to live or buy a car or have the new iPod or whatever. In my life, that hasn't been the key.

Design for Social Impact (now called Social Impact Studios) created this family of logos for the Appel Farm Arts & Music Center, Appel Farm Arts Camp and an online arts communication hub called VirtuARTSity.

Buy Fresh Buy Local is a nationwide initiative to promote fresh and local produce. Design for Social Impact (now called Social Impact Studios) created the national logo and regional versions.

It's that old adage, "Do what you love and the money will come." I don't think it's that the money will come in huge pots. It might come in trickles, it might come slowly, it might not come for a while or it might come later. So, I think what can happen is, if it's not working right away, in this society of instant gratification, with this idea of all or nothing, people can get afraid that it's not going to work.

How many employees do you have?
Right now we're at five. We were up to ten before the economy took a big dive. So, in 2008, we had ten and in 2009 we had to cut our staff down over a period of time. Some of the staff was particular to contracts that we lost as a result of the economy.

How challenging has it been for you to make ends meet for the business?
We make the most of the resources we have. At times, my salary is very small, but my staff's salary is not. I would say that they're making good wages for creative positions. We have full health insurance. My salary is the one that gets flexible when the times get tight. I just have to be creative with it.

Because I have employees and because I have to pay them and pay taxes and pay for

their health care, I hustle. I get out there and I advocate our organization to get them work. I love doing that. I love being out there and increasing our impact. I definitely fit the entrepreneur profile. Entrepreneurs tend to make a go of it at whatever level they're at and they take hits when they need to and they take risks when they need to. But for fifteen years, it has been pretty solid.

Have you ever been approached by a client who doesn't match your mission, but you think, "Gosh, we really need a big project this month"?
That's an interesting question because we never work outside of our mission. But I almost think everybody who's trying to do something positive and believes in what they're doing fits our mission.

Occasionally, people will call us up for something that's just a private interest or wanting a T-shirt designed for their company. It depends on what it is. If it's a small business, if it's woman owned, if it's minority owned, that's already something that's in the field of what we're trying to do. But we never really get requests for something that would bring in enough money that makes me want to go, "Well, I'm going to set aside the mission just once." I've never had to do that.

Now that socially conscious design is a hot topic, has your work life gotten easier or harder?

From a practical level, I know how hard it is to make something like this work. I never feel threatened by people who are doing it because they'll either make it work, and we'll all kind of float our boats, or they may not be able to do this kind of work for the long haul.

One of the benefits is that people have a general concept of social marketing, which is nice because you don't have to describe the importance of identity. People use the word *brand*. We don't use that word. We use *identity* instead.

Why don't you like the word brand?

I feel like a *brand* is something we put onto something else, while *identity* means to come from within. I think there are two parts to identity: It's what you think about yourself and how other people understand you. The concept of branding focuses more on how other people are going to perceive you.

What we really encourage people to do is to be really solid on what they believe they're doing. Because when you believe in what you're doing, you can do anything whether or not you have the resources or the capacity or all the skills. You can really set out to do some amazing things; whereas if you're running after the perception of the outside world, that's only half of the equation. Most of the groups that we work with don't have a lot of budget for repeated advertising and marketing, so they've really got to nail it when they get that one shot out there.

http://socialimpactstudios.com

Ennis Carter and Design for Social Impact (now called Social Impact Studios) created a book called Posters for the People: Art of the WPA. It includes hundreds of historic posters that promote positive social messages instead of products.

MAKE A COMMITMENT TO YOURSELF

Now it's time to turn your passion into action. What one change or project are you going to commit to making a reality?

What's your schedule for making it happen? What will happen today?

This week?

This month?

Use these first steps to create a project plan with a more detailed schedule. We wish you luck, and please keep us posted on your projects!

CONTACT@ALRDESIGN.COM

RESOURCES

Don't want to type in all these links?
Find the free online version of this list here: www.ALRdesign.com/resources.

BLOGS

DESIGN ALTRUISM PROJECT
A high-level discussion about socially conscious design that often acts as a counterpoint to writings, opinions and talks by well-known figures in the design community.
http://design-altruism-project.org

THE GROUNDSWELL BLOG
The companion site to the Groundswell Collective, which focuses on the relationship of art and society, specifically highlighting artists working for social change.
http://groundswellcollective.com

OSOCIO
An amazing and continually growing online collection of social marketing campaigns from across the globe. Get inspired, find out which design approaches work or just discover new issues to care about.
http://osocio.org

REBEL:ART
A constant stream of posts about street art, culture jamming and all sorts of other new activist art. Even though Alain Bieber's site is in German, it's well worth a visit by English speakers since it's pure eye candy and most of its links take you to sites with English explanations, if you need to know more.
www.rebelart.net/diary

SOCIAL DESIGN NOTES
The grandfather of socially conscious design blogs. Spend a Friday afternoon sifting through the archives for hundreds of inspiring posts.
http://backspace.com/notes

SPARE CHANGE: MAKING A DIFFERENCE WITH SOCIAL MARKETING
No, it's not another take on social media marketing. Instead, it's an ongoing discussion of the best marketing techniques for social causes and issues.
http://blog.social-marketing.com

BOOKS

AD NAUSEAM: A SURVIVOR'S GUIDE TO AMERICAN CONSUMER CULTURE (Faber & Faber)
by Carrie McLaren and Jason Torchinsky
A smart and consistently funny critique of consumer culture from the creators of the fantastic and sadly defunct *Stay Free! Magazine*. The book collects articles from the magazine as well as new pieces from both cultural critics and comedians.

THE AGE OF PERSUASION (Counterpoint)
by Terry O'Reilly and Mike Tennant
It's rare to find a book about advertising that both critiques the field while still showing a great deal of love for it at the same time. Through the authors' research and anecdotes from years of working in the business, they paint an insightful and nuanced history of the industry of persuasion.

THE BIG BOOK OF GREEN DESIGN (Harper Design)
by Suzanna MW Stephens and Anthony B. Stephens
More of a coffee table book than a reference manual, but with an intro by Re-Nourish founder Eric Benson, hundreds of visual examples and several detailed case studies, it's an inspiring resource for anyone interested in the environmental direction businesses big and small are taking.

BRANDING FOR NONPROFITS (Allworth Press)
by DK Holland
Filled with plenty of real-world examples and resources, this book should be required reading for any nonprofit interested in harnessing the power of branding (which should really be all of them) and the designers who want to work with them.

CONSCIENTIOUS OBJECTIVES: DESIGNING FOR AN ETHICAL MESSAGE (RotoVision) *by John Cranmer and Yolanda Zappaterra*
A great set of detailed case studies on how designers have worked to further social causes with their design skills. Includes an introduction to the history of design activism by Steven Heller.

CRADLE TO CRADLE (North Point Press)
by William McDonough and Michael Braungart
Cringe every time you toss something in the trash? Read this book for radical ideas about overhauling the life cycle of everyday products, with waste feeding back into production.

CULTURE JAM (Harper Paperbacks) *by Kalle Lasn*
The founder of *Adbusters* magazine takes a critical look at nearly every corner of consumer culture, from TV addiction and brand worship to lack of community.

DEADLY PERSUASION (Free Press)
by Jean Kilbourne
A classic critique of the world of advertising from a feminist perspective. You'll never look at ads the same way after reading it.

DESIGN FOR THE REAL WORLD (Academy Chicago Publishers) *by Victor Papanek*
The original socially conscious design book. Papanek was speaking to industrial designers, but his advice on how to approach design with an ethical perspective is relevant to all design fields and is still pertinent today.

DESIGN IS THE PROBLEM (Rosenfeld Media)
by Nathan Shedroff
A comprehensive overview of the systems available to help designers measure their work's sustainability. Plus, mini case studies on real-world products that are moving in the right direction.

DESIGNING FOR THE GREATER GOOD (Harper Design) *by Peleg Top and Jonathan Cleveland*
Looking for inspiration? This gorgeous look book features page after page of socially conscious design projects along with highly informative case studies.

DO GOOD DESIGN (Peachpit Press)
by David B. Berman
This small volume covers the sins of branding and advertising in a personal, inspirational way. If you're hesitant to commit to design activism, this book offers plenty of reasons to change your mind.

GARBAGE LAND (Little, Brown and Company)
by Elizabeth Royte
An educational and entertaining first-person story of tracking trash. Royte follows all of her own waste through a system that is generally invisible to everyday people and discovers some surprising and upsetting end points.

GOOD: AN INTRODUCTION TO ETHICS IN GRAPHIC DESIGN (AVA Publishing) *by Lucienne Roberts*
An interesting series of interviews with working designers who discuss their approaches to working ethically. It also includes a history of the relationship between ethics and design, as well as a system for designers to map out all the ethical concerns in their field.

GREEN GRAPHIC DESIGN (Allworth Press)
by Brian Dougherty with Celery Design Collaborative
A solid overview of the issues and techniques of environmental graphic design. It features examples from the author's company, Celery Design Collaborative.

NO LOGO (Picador) *by Naomi Klein*
An eye-opening look at the effect of corporate interests on our culture. Rather than an activist rant, it's an incredibly well-researched critique of the rise of branded society. It's even more relevant today than when it came out in 2000.

ORGANIZING FOR SOCIAL CHANGE (Seven Locks Press) *by Kim Bobo, Jackie Kendall and Steve Max*
A practical guide to social activism. While not focused on design, it's a handy guide for people wanting to work outside of the existing systems.

OUR CHOICE: A PLAN TO SOLVE THE CLIMATE CRISIS (Rodale Books) *by Al Gore*
Think of this as the book-length version of Gore's *An Inconvenient Truth*. It takes you behind the science of climate change in an approachable way and offers viable solutions.
http://ourchoicethebook.com/

A PEOPLE'S HISTORY OF THE UNITED STATES (Harper Perennial) *By Howard Zinn*
Want proof that small groups of committed citizens really can make a difference? Read this amazing history of America written from the perspective of working-class men and women.

REALIZING THE IMPOSSIBLE: ART AGAINST AUTHORITY (AK Press)
by Josh Macphee and Erik Reuland
An inspiring overview of artists who have used their skills for the cause of social change throughout history and around the world.

SUSTAINABLE (Rockport Publishers) *by Aaris Sherin*
An invaluable practical handbook on the ins and outs of environmentally conscious graphic design. The book itself was printed using a range of sustainable methods.

THE SWASTIKA: SYMBOL BEYOND REDEMPTION? (Allworth Press) *by Steven Heller*
A history of the now-infamous symbol, which came to be well before the Nazi's made use of it. A fascinating case study on the power of branding.

VOLUNTARY SIMPLICITY (Harper Paperbacks) *by Duane Elgin*
A slim but powerful volume on the importance and benefits of a lifestyle that recognizes the limited resources of our world.

WHY BAD ADS HAPPEN TO GOOD CAUSES
The classic primer on effective advertising for nonprofits, this book offers tons of concrete examples of what works and why. It's no longer in print, but you can download the text for free.
www.agoodmanonline.com/bad_ads_good_causes/

EDUCATION

THE CENTER FOR ART AND COMMUNITY PARTNERSHIPS
This Massachusetts College of Art and Design program pairs students, staff, faculty and alumni with innovative community partnerships.
www.massart.edu/About_MassArt/MassArt_In_the_Community/Center_for_Art_and_Community_Partnerships.html

CREATIVE FOR A CAUSE
A resource for visual communication instructors who want to incorporate social responsibility into their curriculum. Packed with real-world examples.
www.creativeforacause.org

DESIGN FOR SOCIAL INNOVATION MFA
The School of Visual Arts in New York now offers a graduate program that focuses on the tools designers need to become leaders in social innovation.
www.schoolofvisualarts.edu/grad/index.jsp?sid0=2&sid1=447

DESIGNMATTERS
An Art Center College of Design program that challenges students to find design solutions to real-world humanitarian and social problems.
www.designmatters.artcenter.edu

PROJECT M
An unorthodox boot camp of sorts that pushes young designers to explore how they can have a positive impact on the world.
www.projectmlab.com

SVA IMPACT: DESIGN FOR SOCIAL CHANGE
A six-week boot camp on design for social advocacy with separate tracks for social entrepreneurship and client-based efforts.
http://impact.sva.edu

EVENTS, GRANTS AND CONTESTS

AIGA (RE)DESIGNAWARDS
An annual design competition that celebrates sustainable and socially responsible design disciplines ranging from print, packaging and product design to architecture.
www.aigaredesignawards.com

COMPOSTMODERN
AIGA San Francisco puts together this annual conference on sustainable design. The speaker lineup is always impressive, and it has inspired more than one designer to change career paths.
http://compostmodern.org

CURRY STONE DESIGN PRIZE
An annual $100,000 prize for a designer who's helping solve pressing world problems, such as clean air, food and water; shelter; and health care.
http://currystonedesignprize.com

DESIGN GLOBAL CHANGE
A think tank that uses design to create positive change through projects around the world. It started as a course at the University of Hartford.
http://designglobalchange.virb.com

DESIGNERS WITHOUT BORDERS
An organization of designers and design educators that assists groups in the developing world with communications needs.
www.designerswithoutborders.org

THE ENDANGERED SPECIES PRINT PROJECT
A simple idea for activism: Buy a limited-edition print of an endangered species and the money goes to an organization trying to save that animal.
http://endangeredspeciesprintproject.com

FONT AID: THE SOCIETY OF TYPOGRAPHIC AFICIONADOS
To help out with worthwhile causes like the tsunami in Japan, designers contribute work to a collective font that's sold to raise money.
www.typesociety.org/fontaid.html

GOOD50X70
It's a simple yet powerful idea: A group of charities put together creative briefs on global issues. Designers respond to one or more of them with a poster.
http://good50x70.org

THE GRAPHIC IMPERATIVE
This exhibit gathers 121 posters from around the world that address peace, social justice and the environment.
www.thegraphicimperative.org

INSPIRING PROJECTS
Designers Against Monoculture
A mini manifesto for designers to reject the corporate monoculture and work to support the unique cultures of their communities.
www.alrdesign.com/dam.html

JUSTSEEDS
An artist's cooperative that creates work with an activist bent and participates in a variety of collaborative projects.
www.justseeds.org

MAKING PUBLIC POLICY
The Center for Urban Pedagogy's series of downloadable foldout posters show how graphic design can be used to better explain public policy.
www.makingpolicypublic.net

POSTER FOR TOMORROW
An international poster contest that focuses on a different human rights theme each year. Take a look at the galleries of past submissions for a big dose of inspiration.
www.posterfortomorrow.org

POSTERS FOR THE PEOPLE
An impressive collection of Works Progress Administration (WPA) posters. Browse the online gallery or buy the book.
www.postersforthepeople.com

POWER TO THE POSTER
A large bank of protest posters for anyone to use. As one of the site's slogans says, "download, print and R.I.P. (rally in peace)."
www.powertotheposter.org

PROJECT H DESIGN
An ongoing series of design initiatives that focus on humanity, habitats, health, happiness and more. Headed up by Emily Pilloton.
www.projecthdesign.org

SAPPI IDEAS THAT MATTER
The name says it all: Apply for a grant (they range from $5,000 to $50,000) to create a project for a nonprofit with the potential to create positive change.
www.na.sappi.com/ideasthatmatterNA/index.html

SOCIALDESIGNSITE.COM
Browse this impressive collection of social design projects to get inspired by all the innovative projects already happening around the world.
www.socialdesignsite.com

MOVIES & VIDEO

AFFLUENZA
A hard look at overconsumption in America and the toll it takes on the environment and our lives. Don't miss the sequel: Escape From Affluenza.
www.pbs.org/kcts/affluenza

COPYRIGHT CRIMINALS
A documentary on music sampling and its uncomfortable relationship with copyright law.
www.copyrightcriminals.com

THE CORPORATION
A harsh critique of the growing power that corporations wield in our society.
www.thecorporation.com

FAIR(Y) USE TALE
A critical look at copyright law and fair use made up entirely of clips from Disney movies.
www.youtube.com/watch?v=CJn_jC4FNDo

FREEDOCUMENTARIES.ORG
Stream a wide variety of compelling, full-length documentaries for free, from Michael Moore's Sicko to The Tobacco Conspiracy.
http://freedocumentaries.org

LIFE AND DEBT
A documentary that show the real impacts of globalization on a developing country.
www.lifeanddebt.org

THE PERSUADERS
A FRONTLINE documentary that takes a look at how marketing and advertising affect how we act, what we buy and how we view the world and ourselves.
www.pbs.org/wgbh/pages/frontline/shows/persuaders/view/

THE STORY OF STUFF PROJECT
A series of compelling videos that reveal troubling truths about the production of stuff, from bottled water to cosmetics.
www.storyofstuff.com

TARGET WOMEN
A blisteringly funny look at how the media markets to women. Be prepared to snort coffee out your nose.
http://current.com/shows/infomania/target-women/

THE YES MEN
Artist/activists Andy Bichlbaum and Mike Bonanno use their creative skills to impersonate representatives of corporations in elaborate pranks that draw attention to political issues that might not otherwise get media coverage. Their "identity corrections" have been documented in two films, and they continue to make appearances in places you least expect them.
http://theyesmen.org

RADIO

THE AGE OF PERSUASION
In this entertaining Canadian radio show, an advertising industry insider takes a lovingly critical look at the history of commercial persuasion.
www.cbc.ca/ageofpersuasion

WEBSITES AND TOOLS

B CORPORATION
In this modified corporate structure, the B stands for beneficial, and companies who bear the letter must live up to transparent standards for social and environmental conduct.
www.bcorporation.net

Certified
B
Corporation
bcorporation.net

CREATIVE COMMONS
An alternative to copyright that lets creators set different levels of acceptable sharing for their intellectual property.
http://CreativeCommons.org

DESIGN CAN CHANGE
A crash course in major environmental issues and the power graphic designers have to make a positive impact.
www.designcanchange.org

THE DESIGNERS ACCORD
A coalition of designers and leaders working toward positive environmental and social change. The website is chock-full of inspiring stories, resources and news.
www.designersaccord.org

EATING GREEN CALCULATOR
Wonder how your food choices impact the planet? Just answer a few simple questions and this handy tool will calculate your diet's environmental footprint.
www.cspinet.org/EatingGreen/calculator.html

FOREST STEWARDSHIP COUNCIL
Learn everything there is to know about FSC paper—where it comes from, what the certification means and more—straight from the source.
www.fsc.org

GRAPHIC WITNESS
A vast collection of art and design used in service of social commentary and a terrific resource for catching up on your socially conscious design history.
www.graphicwitness.org

THE LIVING PRINCIPLES
A wealth of resources and stories about using design as a tool for positive change.
www.livingprinciples.org

NIELSEN'S MYBESTSEGMENTS
A look at how the marketing and advertising worlds segment and target consumers. Click on "Free Report" and enter your zip code to see the break down on your neighborhood.
www.mybestsegments.com

RE-NOURISH
A one-stop online resource that helps designers reduce their environmental impact: case studies, a calculator for reducing paper waste, independent info on environmentally responsible printing and paper choices, and more.
www.re-nourish.com

THEY RULE
A visual look at the people who run some of the biggest corporations in the United States and how they're connected to each other. It's a truly eye-opening look at how a few hands hold the power.
www.theyrule.net

CONTRIBUTORS

Citizen Research & Design
New York, New York
http://citizenrd.com

Clif Bar & Company
Emeryville, California
www.clifbar.com

Lincoln Cushing
Author and lecturer
Berkeley, California
www.docspopuli.org

Design Action Collective
Oakland, California
http://designaction.org

Design for Social Impact
Philadelphia, Pennsylvania
http://socialimpactstudios.com/

John Emerson
Designer, writer, activist
New York, New York
www.backspace.com

Free Range Studios
Berkeley, California,
and Washington DC
www.freerange.com

goodgood
Boston, Massachusetts
www.goodgoodland.com

Daniel Green
Designer
Green Bay, WI

Greener Media
New York, New York
http://greenermedia.com

Johnson & Johnson
Global Strategic Design Office
New York, New York
www.jnj.com

JusticeDesign
San Francisco, California
www.justicedesign.com

Justseeds
Various locations
http://justseeds.org

Liberty Science Center
Jersey City, New Jersey
http://lsc.org

LeAnn Locher & Associates
Portland, Oregon
www.leannlocher.com

Mark & Phil
Poughkeepsie, New York
http://markandphil.com

Mended Arrow Design
Richmond, Virginia
www.mendedarrow.com

Metro Los Angeles
Los Angeles, California
www.metro.net

Merck
Whitehouse Station, New Jersey
www.merck.com

Milton Glaser Inc.
New York, New York
www.miltonglaser.com

MSLK
Long Island City, New York
www.mslk.com

The Public
Toronto, Canada
www.thepublicstudio.ca

Raised Eyebrow
Vancouver, Canada
www.raisedeyebrow.com

Rogue Element
Chicago, Illinois
www.rogue-element.com

re:active, Inc.
Portland, Oregon
www.reactivemagazine.com

Jess Sand
Designer and activist
http://sustainabledesignlabs.org

Studio Sonda
Croatia
www.sonda.hr

Squishy Press
Chicago, Illinois
www.squishypress.com

UnderConsideration LLC
Austin, Texas
www.underconsideration.com

James Victore Inc.
New York, New York
www.jamesvictore.com/

Nathan Wessel
Activist and urban planning student
Cincinnati, Ohio
www.kickstarter.com/
profile/1057319855

Worldstudio
New York, New York
www.worldstudioinc.com

ABOUT

Based in Richmond, Virginia, Noah Scalin is an artist and designer, and founder of the socially conscious design and consulting firm Another Limited Rebellion. A lifelong activist, his first protest marches were spent in a stroller and then on roller skates. A former art director for independent movie studio Troma Entertainment and international clothing company Avirex, Noah used his experience with youth marketing and passion for grassroots activism to create his own ethically driven firm in 2001.

He's also an adjunct faculty member at Virginia Commonwealth University where he teaches Design Rebels, a course he created on socially conscious graphic design. Noah's fine art has been exhibited internationally and his award-winning project Skull-A-Day (www.SkullADay.com) was the subject of his first book: *Skulls*. His recent books include *365: A Daily Creativity Journal* and *Unstuck: 52 Ways to Get (and Keep) Your Creativity Flowing at Home, at Work and in Your Studio*. **www.NoahScalin.com**

THE AUTHORS

Michelle Taute is a writer and content strategist with more than a decade of experience. She creates compelling copy for magazines, blogs, websites, scrappy entrepreneurs and really big brands. A regular contributor to *HOW* magazine, Michelle's articles have appeared everywhere from *Better Homes and Gardens* and *Woman's Day* specials to *Metropolis* and *USA Weekend*.

Michelle edits *I.D.*'s social media presence and for the past two years, she's organized the prestigious I.D. Annual Design Review competition. Michelle is the author of *Design Matters: Brochures*, and when she's not crafting copy for clients, you might find her obsessively making paper fortune tellers for her blog, The Daily Cootie Catcher: http:paperfortunetellers.com. Keep up with this Cincinnati, Ohio, writer's latest projects at **www.michelletaute.com**.

THE INDEX

ARTWORK CREDITS

MORE GREAT TITLES FROM HOW BOOKS

JUST DESIGN:
SOCIALLY CONSCIOUS DESIGN FOR CRITICAL CAUSES

By Christopher Simmons

For many, doing good work that also does good in the world is part of the ethos of design practice. Just Design celebrates and explores this increasingly critical aspect of design by showcasing a diverse collection of inspiring projects, people and causes.

DAMN GOOD:
TOP DESIGNERS DISCUSS THEIR ALL-TIME FAVORITE PROJECTS

By Tim Lapetino and Jason Adam

Highlighting some of the best work of designers around the globe, this unique and diverse collection challenges the status quo and typical industry boundaries, and also contains the stories behind the work—in the words of the creative teams who designed them.

 For more news, tips and articles, follow us at Twitter.com/HOWbrand

 For behind-the-scenes information and special offers, become a fan at Facebook.com/HOWmagazine

 For visual inspiration, follow us at Pinterest.com/HOWbrand

FIND THESE BOOKS AND MANY OTHERS AT MYDESIGNSHOP.COM OR YOUR LOCAL BOOKSTORE.